ROUTE

66

FROM TARBOLTON TO TOXTETH
VIA TOULOUSE

ALAN MCKINNELL

FAITH BUILDERS

Faithbuilders Publishing
12 Dukes Court, Bognor Road, Chichester, PO19 8FX, United Kingdom
www.faithbuilderspublishing.com

ISBN: 978-1-913181-66-6

You can contact the author via email using: alanjeanroute66@gmail.com; www.alanjeanroute66.com

Cover design by Esther Kotecha, EKDesigns
Layout by Faithbuilders Publishing
Printed in the United Kingdom

Contents

In the beginning was the Word, and the Word was with God, and the Word was God. He was with God in the beginning. Through him all things were made; without him nothing was made that has been made. In him was life, and that life was the light of all mankind. The light shines in the darkness, and the darkness has not overcome it.

There was a man sent from God whose name was John. He came as a witness to testify concerning that light, so that through him all might believe. He himself was not the light; he came only as a witness to the light.

The true light that gives light to everyone was coming into the world. He was in the world, and though the world was made through him, the world did not recognise him. He came to that which was his own, but his own did not receive him.

Yet to all who did receive him, to those who believed in his name, he gave the right to become children of God – children born not of natural descent, nor of human decision or a husband's will, but born of God.

The Word became flesh and made his dwelling among us. We have seen his glory, the glory of the one and only Son, who came from the Father, full of grace and truth.

John 1 (NIV)

Introduction

Sometime in 1999 I became a Christian; I say sometime because it took me some time to get it.

It was the start of a new life in which I have experienced every emotion but boredom. If your life as a Christian is not challenging and exciting, then I challenge you to get excited. If you are not living an adventure then, like me in the beginning, you probably have not got it yet, or to be more precise you definitely have not got Him, Jesus, yet. My wife by the way 'got it' straight away, women can be so annoying!

Route 66 has always been my thing, hence the title, and in 2004 my wife and I drove it, giving out homemade tracts. But more of that later.

I always wanted to write a book with Route 66 in the title, not very original I know but, as I had driven Route 66, I thought I had a bit more right to use it than others who have not driven it. Oh and no, I did not do it on a Harley Davidson, we did it in a Dodge Grand Caravan. If you have ever driven Route 66 and it comes up in conversation (which it does) there is generally someone who has not driven it, trying to demean what you have done by asking, 'did you do it on a Harley?', as if driving 2,700 miles across the good old US of A was not something enough to be treasured. Well, I have been there, done that and bought the fridge magnets, Harley or no Harley.

My wife and I have so many stories of God's grace, His mercy, His love, His provision and His patience, that we felt it right to write them down, or rather that I should right them down. I went to university for the first time at the age of fifty and loved it. I loved researching (or rather sitting in the library reading more and more faith books) and then putting it down on paper. It was a great time, but since graduating in 2011 with an MA in Theology and Religious Studies (not as boring as it sounds) I have never written another thing. But now, armed with my first laptop at the age of 56 I am going to give it a go. I am not writing to be published but to be obedient, I believe God has called me to write this book, maybe just for myself and maybe because I do not count my blessings enough, (do you?) but I am just going to enjoy myself and see what happens. I have put it off for long enough now and so I am just going to start writing and see where it leads.

I wondered about the possibility of writing a book which in all probability would be just short stories, then I thought on 66 stories, but who writes books with 66 short chapters? So I kept praying for inspiration. Then, one day I bought a book in the Christian bookshop in Birkenhead, it was reduced, so being a 'canny Scotsman' I bought it, my deep theological reasoning in buying the book was that it was cheap. On reading it, I felt the Lord challenging me to count the chapters; they were not numbered, only titled, so I started counting them, and yes there were 66 chapters. So, it was possible to write a book with 66 small chapters. (I've just checked again, definitely 66 chapters, I didn't count the 'Thanks to' and the 'Postscript' sections.) You can check this out for yourself, the book is called *Through the Pilgrim Door*, (a great title, another reason I bought the book) by Michael Volland. So, I announced this 'sign' to my wife and, as wives do, she reminded me of it several weeks later and asked me what I was doing about it.

So here I am, prompted by the Holy Spirit and nudged by a Holy wife eventually getting down to writing who knows what for who knows who... so here goes...

You Must Be Born Again

Jesus answered and said to him, "Most assuredly, I say to you, unless one is born again, he cannot see the kingdom of God." John 3:3

I suppose if we are going to take a journey then we should start at the beginning. (The beginning of a new life.)

You must be Born Again.

I was not really looking for anything more in my life, I had kind of settled for life as it was, warts (rather big warts) and all, and besides, looking for more is always dangerous in so many different ways. It only leads to dissatisfaction; better to put up and shut up and make the best of what life had given you. To be fair, at this time in my life I had my fair share of good. I had a lovely wife and young daughter, we were living in South-west France, where I had a good job. We lived in a detached villa with a swimming pool and I drove a 4 Litre Toyota Landcruiser (paid for in cash) with more chrome on it than you could imagine.

We had holidays when and wherever we liked and we were living the good life, on the surface.

Then it happened. My wife Jean found Jesus, or rather Jesus found her.

We had just had our barny to end all barnies. We had been out drinking (there's a surprise) and when we came home Jean started on about me and other women. When I had been drinking, I thought I was God's gift, the life and soul of the party and I had to have everyone's attention, usually women's. As Jean challenged me about it, I just exploded; this was a pattern with me, I would go along stuffing down my anger and keeping it 'under control' then bang, the volcano would erupt. We had just spent a small fortune on having decorators in, usually I did my own decorating but our living room was two stories high with a mezzanine level, the decorators brought scaffolding with them. I started throwing bottles of red wine against the walls and jumping on the phone and generally smashing things up. I had smashed up every home we had ever been in. This was to be the last. Over the next few days, we set about making repairs to the house. One of my friends was coming out that week to stay and Jean's parents were due the following week. I had to put wood panelling on one wall, while Jean washed walls and floors and I touched up another wall. One particular wall, I put up a fake light switch to cover up a hole that I had made when smashing a bottle off it. It was the last straw, when we came out to France Jean had determined that things were going to change, or else. But nothing had changed. Jean was at the end of herself and determined to take our daughter back to Scotland and start again, even if it meant giving up all this life of luxury to stay in a council flat somewhere, she just could not take it anymore. But God.

Now my wife Jean has never been one for watching TV, so that the following happening is nothing short of a miracle and was to be the first in a long line of God taking us and guiding us to a new relationship, with Him through His Son Jesus and with each other.

While standing ironing in our living room she was flicking through the channels on TV. We had taken Sky TV out to France with us in order that we might have some English-speaking TV to watch but we never watched it much, we were usually too busy drinking and partying. This day however, Jean was drawn to a Channel with 'GOD' up in the corner of the screen and she stopped and wondered what it was all about. There was a man on who said, 'there is someone out there who is desperate and what you need in your life is Jesus Christ.' She was drawn to the front of the TV set and got down on her knees and prayed a prayer with that man, not having a clue as to what she was doing. The man said she now had to do three things: read her Bible every day, talk to Jesus every day, and join a good Bible teaching church.

Jean went outside to our garden and standing by our pool she knew that things were never going to be the same again. She came to a realisation of where our marriage really was, dead and going nowhere.

Looking back, Jean realised it had been dead for some time and she saw no way forward. Jean went into our garage and somehow, in among all the boxes she managed to find the Bible we had been given on our wedding day, 17 years before, kept as a keepsake, a memento, never realising that one day it would be used to save and restore our marriage.

I thought she had 'flipped it.' It was going to be a long painful journey, but no pain, no gain, and we were about to gain so much more than we ever imagined.

So Jesus answered and said, "Assuredly, I say to you, there is no one who has left house or brothers or sisters or father or mother or children or lands, for My sake and the gospel's, who shall not receive a hundredfold now in this time—houses and brothers and sisters and mothers and children and lands, with persecutions—and in the age to come, eternal life. (Mark 10:29-30)

In The Beginning

In the Beginning God...... Genesis 1 v 1
In the beginning was the Word........John 1 v 1
God and the Word...... together in the beginning

*In the beginning **God** created the heavens and the earth. The earth was without form, and void; and darkness was on the face of the deep. And **the Spirit of God** was hovering over the face of the waters. **Then God said, "Let there be light"**; and there was light. And God saw the light that it was good; and God divided the light from the darkness. God called the light Day, and the darkness He called Night. So the evening and the morning were the first day.* Genesis 1 v 1 - 5

The Holy Trinity appears on the very first day of creation, all three were there in the beginning; God the Father, God the Holy Spirit and God the Son. **God**, **the Spirit of God**, and **God said**, (God's Word, 'the Word became flesh' Jesus: John 1:14)

Every story has a beginning, and every story has its characters but not all the characters are there at the beginning of the story, characters tend to come and go with just the main characters there throughout the story, whether actually or implied. God the Father, God the Son and God the Holy Spirit are the main characters in our life stories (and you thought it was you) whether actually or implied, whether acknowledged or ignored, whether we believe or not. The rest of the characters we meet come and go along the way but the defining characters in our life stories stay, whether physically or in our hearts, and they are added to along the way.

My name is Alan, I was born in 1959, I married Jean in 1982, our daughter Kerry was born in 1986, she married Andrew in 2009, and they have two sons, Rufus, born in 2015 and Axel, born in 2018. Right now, they are the main characters in our lives. We both have parents, sisters, brothers, brothers-in-law and a variety of friends, work colleagues and a whole host of people who have played a part in our lives, but in this book we are going to concentrate on the main player in our lives, someone who was always there but who we didn't recognise or acknowledge until it was almost too late; that someone was and is Jesus Christ. Without whom our story would have a different ending, but God.

My wife and I were born and brought up in the same small village of Tarbolton in Scotland where we met when she was only 13. I would love to say it was love at first sight, that we started going out as childhood sweethearts and never looked back, but it did not happen that way. I always say that Jean was thirteen when I first asked her out and she was sixteen when she said yes, unfortunately I was 19 and already had some skewed ideas about love.

We started dating and we got married when Jean was just 19. The fact that we are still together after all these years is only by the grace of God and the perseverance of a good woman, strengthened and empowered by her love of Jesus Christ, and the indwelling of the Holy Spirit. Now if all of this 'religiously' sounding talk is gobbledegook to you then don't worry it was gobbledegook to me for most of my life too, particularly the first forty years.

I was brought up Church of Scotland, nothing wrong with that but it didn't mean a lot to me, all I knew was that my best friend, the minister's son, didn't get out to play on a Sunday. I went to Sunday school as a boy and even in my early teens but by then I had other things on my mind, girls. I was a Boy Scout, and we ran a disco in the Scout Hall and so my fascination with girls began; nothing unusual in that for a teenage boy but as I got older my liking for a drink, followed by chasing girls meant that I did not learn to develop proper relationships with girls. I never took time to get to know them, and if things were not going along as I liked then I would just date someone else, without the courtesy of calling it off with the first girl. I was getting older and still running the disco with my friends but the girls I were dating were not getting older. Had I not met Jean when I did, things could have got a whole lot messier. I just didn't show any respect to the girls I was dating, and the sad part was I called it 'love'. Love that involved Alan taking all he could get and giving nothing in return, expecting girls just to be grateful that I had shown an interest, but leaving a wake of disillusioned young girls. A love language that was going to carry on into my marriage, a long way into my marriage. Now if any of the girls I dated at the time ever get to read this, and I don't really see how they will, but anyway I would just like to say how truly sorry I am for the way I treated you, I was wrong, I was horrible and I was totally self-centred, please forgive me.

Throughout our marriage right up until we became committed Christians my whole view of life was one of selfishness and pride. Selfishly serving myself while expecting my wife to be happy with her lot. Then, as I started making more and more money, Jean was expected to be grateful for such a good provider and to overlook all the other drunken nonsense that was going on. Unfortunately, Jean and I were 'drinking partners' from the beginning and it got worse and worse as we tried to fill the empty voids in our lives created by lack of a wholesome outlook on love, especially on my part. Even when our daughter, who I love deeply, was born, the whole concept of love didn't get me. That there could be more to love than just buying things and taking my family places, places that always had a bar, just did not register with me. I thought I was a nice guy, oh dear. I always said, if I ever write my story I'm going to call it 'No More Mister Nice Guy.' There is one thing for sure, nice guy I was not.

Call It Like It Is – Adultery

"You have heard that it was said to those of old, 'You shall not commit adultery.' But I say to you that whoever looks at a woman to lust for her has already committed adultery with her in his heart.
Matthew 5 v 27-28.

No one likes the thought of being in adultery. We may have a fling or an extra marital affair or we may even convince ourselves that we were 'only looking' and there is no harm in that, but Jesus, in Matthew 5 v 27-28, makes it quite clear that there is harm in looking, because Jesus knows that once it takes root in your heart there is only one place it's going and that's downwards. You may never get around to committing adultery, but your heart is heading in the wrong direction, a direction that is taking you away from your wife.

The day I committed adultery was not the lowest point in my life, that came in the next couple of days as I tried to lie and squirm my way out of it. I did not want to admit that I had become who I had become but the truth wasn't going anywhere and the pit I was digging was getting deeper and deeper. It is amazing how low you can go to try and protect what you have just chosen to trash.

We had been at a Christmas night out and three couples ended up at a friend's house, we all decided to stay as we lived in different towns. One by one, everyone crashed out until I was left alone with my friend's wife in the kitchen. This led to me making advances to her and we kissed; as soon as it happened it couldn't be taken back. It was once, but it was life destroying and led to the worst time in my life. I had betrayed my wife, a woman who loved and trusted me, and it was about to get worse as I tried to cover it up in the hope that it would all just go away. But sin does not 'just go away', it has consequences, life changing consequences, and not being a Christian yet I had no idea how to deal with this other than more sin to cover it up.

The next morning, my wife knew something had happened but she didn't say anything until we got home. I tried to blame my friend, saying he was up to his old tricks, but Jean knew this wasn't what happened, and she threatened to go to our friends, confront them and find out the truth. I eventually owned up to kissing her, I said it was nothing it was only a kiss. That was probably the worst thing I could have said. I had betrayed my wife with another woman and now I was saying it was nothing. I dug a bigger and bigger hole for myself as I tried to make out that I wasn't that bad a man, but the truth was I was rotten to the core and I had just proved it: adultery and cheating and then lying and finger pointing to save my own skin without a thought to my wife. My thinking seemed to be that if I could bring what I had done to something less than what I had actually done, then the hurt would be less that what actually it was and that we could just go on as if it never happened. But it had happened, Jean was hurting and I was only turning the knife in the wound in my self-centred attempt at self-preservation.

It would take years and God to mend the hurt and it would only start for real when Jesus 'slapped' me into the kingdom.

I started a new job in France in July 1996, we were still hiding in alcohol and when Jean got saved through watching God TV I thought she had flipped it and wanted nothing to do with Christianity. I threw the Bible at Jean and said there was nothing in it for me, it was written by clever men, as if not only did I not need God, I didn't even need very clever men to help me.

Then one night, I took a Bible with me to work. I opened it and the first verses God showed me was Matthew 5 v 27 – 29.

"You have heard that it was said to those of old, 'You shall not commit adultery.' But I say to you that whoever looks at a woman to lust for her has already committed adultery with her in his heart. If your right eye causes you to sin, pluck it out and cast it from you; for it is more

profitable for you that one of your members perish, than for your whole body to be cast into hell.

I had always been an adulterer at heart and it inevitably led to adultery. I went home and showed Jean the verses God had shown me and repented; it was the start of our healing. It would be a long journey but one that would lead to complete healing, a new marriage and a new life, a new life made possible by a loving Father God, the grace of His Son Jesus Christ and the power of the Holy Spirit.

4

Toulouse – The High Life

*For I know the plans I have for you,' declares the Lord, 'plans to
prosper you and not to harm you, plans to give you hope and a future.*
Jeremiah 29:11 (NIVUK)

When we arrived in Toulouse, France on the 1st of July 1996 I received
a settling in bonus of £10,000 as well as an increase in salary, a shift
allowance, a hire car, rent paid for up to three years and sunshine;
what more could anyone ask for? We needed to start again, and I
thought money was going to be our answer. Even though money had
never been a problem in Scotland, somehow more of it was going to
help. All our problems would be left behind in Scotland.

Starting all over seems the answer, and in many ways it is, but you can
only start again if you have finished the previous journey, if you have
dealt with your old life, repented of it and then moved on. That was
something that I still hadn't got a hold of, I was going to do it 'My Way'.
More than twenty years later I still meet so many people, men in
particular, who want to do it their way, and they wonder why they are
stuck in a rut. 'Regrets I've had a few' - the longer you go on those 'few
regrets' keep adding up, unless you deal with them. Sweeping
everything under the carpet may work for a while, but sooner or later
you will trip over the carpet and the more mess you have under there
then the bigger the fall that is coming. I had a lot of mess and I had a
big fall coming. But I was oblivious to it, I was in a new job, in a new
country and it was going to be just fine, let's open another bottle and
start partying. I never thought for a minute that that was where I had
left off, and that that was where my problems came from. So not only
was I not dealing with my past, I was moving straight into doing the
same thing I had previously been doing and hoping that I was going to

have different results. As the saying goes, "Only a fool keeps doing the same thing and expects different results."

The job I got in France was completely new to me. I had been turned down for the job twice in Scotland previously because I wasn't an engineer, but now here I was in France doing it.

Prior to getting the job in France I worked at British Aerospace in Prestwick, Scotland. The factory was five miles from our home village of Tarbolton and by 1996 we were living in a house in Ayr, about seven miles from our home village and about three miles from the factory. We were not well travelled folk. The opportunity came up to go to France when I applied for a job in the Customer Support department and got it. It then transpired that there were not enough jobs to go around and that I was being dropped. This after announcing to everyone we were going to France and Jean having given up her job. We were devastated. I complained and was told there was nothing they could do about it. I still had my job at Prestwick and should be grateful for that. I pressed on and one day I called the Customer Support Director to complain; his stance was 'do you have anything in writing' which I hadn't. He said there were only three jobs left and I wasn't suitable for any of them. I asked what they were, he said, Sales Director, I agreed I couldn't do that, Technical Liaison Engineer, I agreed I couldn't do that, then he said AOG desk, I said I could do that. The push was on. I had been turned down for this position twice while it was in Prestwick because I was not an engineer, but I knew I could do it and that the prerequisite of being an engineer was something that the engineers in Prestwick held to and not something they used on the job. I ended up on 'Mahogany Row' (the nickname for the offices of the top directors) in the office of the CEO stating my case. He said to me the job is yours and we were on our way. God had a plan, and I was not even aware of Him (yet).

I was excited that we were heading to France, to a new life in the sunshine. I didn't even know what the wages were, what the bonuses were, where we would live, what I would drive, how schools for Kerry would work out, what would Jean do all day in a foreign country with me at work and Kerry at school, we were just off. Looking back, it is obvious I was running from something, there was an element of desperation in the move, but I was still so oblivious to who I was and what I was really like. I had a mask on and the person who believed in the mask more than anyone else was, you've guessed it, me. Looking back, I honestly believe that had we not gone to France I would have lived with the mask and through that lost everything, not money or jobs, but Jean and Kerry. The only things that at the end of the day really matter are not things, they are your loved ones. The people you share life with and unfortunately the people you are most able to hurt. I was still carrying on like a freight train, full steam ahead, not seeing the brick wall that was coming.

Within six months of arriving in Toulouse we had purchased our own house, a large five-bedroom house, with a huge living room and dining area, a mezzanine area, a large dining kitchen with breakfast bar, private gardens, two garages and a swimming pool. I used my £10,000 bonus to pay cash for a 4 Litre Toyota Landcruiser, LWB. We had various other settling in bonuses and a good wage to boot. We had arrived. Only thing is, no matter where you go to get away from your problems, you are going to be there, and as most of our problems are ourselves then we never arrive anywhere new until we deal with the old. God was going to do it, but it was all going to take time and get a bit messy. The first thing was facing reality and it wasn't going to be me doing that, it all started when Jean got saved and that was going to be two years down the line and then another eighteen months of me struggling with coming to terms with life as it really was. Only Jesus was going to be able to help me with that one, the good thing is 'I fought the Lord, and the Lord won.'

I always say that the thing that nearly stopped me from becoming a Christian was that I did not want to look deep inside and see who I really was and what I was really like. But that was what was ultimately going to set me free and only Jesus gives you the strength to do that.

Therefore if the Son makes you free, you shall be free indeed.
(John 8:36)

5

Chemin des Anes

Then the Lord opened the donkey's mouth. Numbers 22:28

One day as Jean kept trying to speak to me about Jesus and the Bible I had had enough. I told her that there was nothing in it (the Bible) for me, it was written by clever men. Now having rejected that it was written by God I did seem to be acknowledging that it was written by clever men, so to say that there was nothing in it for me I was saying that clever men could not teach me anything. That, to say the least, was being a bit on the arrogant side, but then again that was me.

I picked up the dog's lead, got the dog and stormed out the house. I just kept walking and eventually came to the outskirts of the small village we were living in in France, Pibrac. I came across a woodland walk which I was unaware of and started walking around it.

God would use this walk for Jean and me to walk round and battle with all the garbage that God wanted us to deal with. It was a quiet and peaceful setting. That was about to change. It was called, appropriately enough 'Chemin des Anes' the Way of the Donkeys. I say appropriately enough because my stubbornness had and would continue to give us grief. Why do I hold so much importance to being right? Or to being justified by my own ways? Self-centredness, pride, clinging to the hope that my life had some meaning and that it wasn't just a sham.

Probably all of the above. It is only when we lay down our lives and we pick up the cross of Jesus that the past stops having a hold on us, but that laying it down just seems so hard because it means trusting in someone other than ourselves. My life may have been a mess, but it was my mess, I got me into it and I would get me out of it... wrong.

The pressures of trying to sort out my life the way I thought it should be done and not the way God wanted to do it became too great. Jesus says in Matthew 11:29-30

Take My yoke upon you and learn from Me, for I am gentle and lowly in heart, and you will find rest for your souls. For My yoke is easy and My burden is light." Instead of yoking myself to Jesus I was still yoking myself to myself, a stubborn donkey.

One day when I was driving home, I stopped the car at a junction and hesitated. My wife Jean said to me 'What's wrong?' I said 'I don't know where I am'. She said, 'There's our house there'. You could see from the car quite clearly where our house was, yet I did not know where I was. Jean asked if this had happened before, and I said yes once before. I ended up going to see a psychiatrist in France. I spoke to him for about 20 or 30 mins, he wrote me a prescription and told me to come back and see him in a month. Meanwhile, we went for prayer and counselling with our minister, Rev. Laurie Mort, and his wife, Miriam.

When I went back to the psychiatrist I had been speaking to him for about 5 minutes when he stopped me and said, 'You're better, I can see it in your eyes', there was a look of amazement on his face as he continued, 'The last time I saw you, you weren't here, today you are here'. He wrote me another prescription and handed it to me. I left his office that day knowing it was God who had healed me through prayer, I stopped taking the tablets, never went back to see the psychiatrist again and never looked back. Fully trusting in God as it says in Philippians 1:6:

being confident of this very thing, that He who has begun a good work in you (me) will complete it until the day of Jesus Christ;

Jean and I continued to walk round that walk for over year doing it God's way. God promised that He would leave no stone unturned, and some of the stuff hiding under the stones I would have left unturned, but God's ways are higher than our ways, and His ways produce life, an abundant life.

I have come that they may have life, and that they may have it more abundantly. John 10:10

He brings us from darkness into light, and He brings our dark deeds into the light, not to expose us or to shame us, but so that we can be set free from them.

Therefore if the Son makes you free, you shall be free indeed.
John 8:36

If we want to be truly free, we have to let the light of Jesus shine in our hearts and then walk in that light; we can never do it on our own, we will always keep something back lest we feel we will be thought less of, but God alone knows the way to true freedom.

For you were once darkness, but now you are light in the Lord. Walk as children of light. Ephesians 5:8

Laurie

But you, O man of God, flee these things and pursue righteousness, godliness, faith, love, patience, gentleness. 1 Timothy 6:11

I have found that while God is the one who changes hearts by the grace and mercy shown to us through His son Jesus and enables us to grow through the empowerment of His Holy Spirit, God will often work through a man or woman of God and at just the right time He will have just the right person or persons there for you. Laurie and his wife Miriam were just that for us, the right godly couple who showed us 'righteousness, godliness, faith, love, patience, gentleness', enabling us to see the love of God reaching out to us. He was Church of England and she was Roman Catholic, any previous prejudices I had (being a Protestant from the west of Scotland) were being washed away right at the beginning of my journey.

We had been saved now for almost six months and had not been to church, well we were in a foreign country and did not speak the language, when I got my works newsletter which contained an advert for the 'English Speaking Church of Toulouse'. So, the excuse for not speaking the language went out the window. I showed the advert to Jean and said, 'I think we should go there.' We agreed but how were we going to go about it? Sunday morning had always been 'lie and die day', the morning after the night before, although by the time we were in France we avoided hangovers by staying drunk. But now we were living differently and so Sunday mornings (when I wasn't working) had become available. Our memories of attending church were wearing your 'Sunday best', so we went and got some new clothes. I had to get a new jacket as I did not have one, and we dressed Kerry up in a nice dress and some black patent shoes. We were off. But not before Jean went through a traumatic battle. She had been living behind alcohol for years now and did not do going out in public, especially without some Dutch courage. It was later on that she confessed to me that prior to leaving the house she had been on her knees to God saying she couldn't do this. But God told her He would take her by her right hand and would never leave her or forsake her.

For I, the Lord your God, will hold your right hand, Saying to you, 'Fear not, I will help you.' Isaiah 41:13

We went to church and as soon as it was over, we slipped out the back and got into our car and headed off. Just as we were leaving the car park this man in white robes came running up to us, robes flowing. It was the minister, Laurie, he wanted to come and see us and so we gave him our address and sped off. During this first service Laurie had preached that 'you know some of you out there look so good on the outside (in our Sunday best) but in the inside you are miserable and dying: that was us. After another five or six Sundays I said to Jean on the way home 'there must be someone else needing a message' I felt that they were all for me. She said, 'No Alan, you need them all.' God had us in just the right place.

Laurie's full name was Rev. Laurie Mort, an unfortunate name for a vicar in France, Mort being French for 'death', but he certainly helped bring the life of Christ into our lives and marriage. From the first time he came to our house sitting by the pool, until we left France for Bible college in England, Laurie and his wife Miriam were good friends and 'Holy Spirit' counsellors to us. They helped guide us through eighteen months of 'heart surgery' as God left no stone unturned.

On one occasion when we were in their house and I was receiving ministry and prayer from Laurie, I could feel his hand on my shoulder. I opened my eyes and Laurie's hands were in front of him, but I knew there was a hand on my shoulder, I could feel the warmth of it. You can make of that what you like but I know what I felt, and I know it was real.

Laurie went on to encourage us to get involved in the church, running prayer meetings and Alpha courses in our house. We remain forever grateful for the time and love they poured into such 'a wretch like us'.

It was a kick start to our faith journey which still goes on today, 20 years later.

The last we heard of Laurie he had left the ministry, a great loss to the church but we fully expect he is still ministering somewhere to those he meets. We are heading back to Toulouse for my 60th birthday and will be trying to look him up, hopefully he will still be in the area; his wife is French so he may still be around somewhere. God willing, we will find them.

To Tithe or Not to Tithe

"Will a man rob God? Yet you have robbed Me! But you say, 'In what way have we robbed You?' In tithes and offerings. You are cursed with a curse, for you have robbed Me, Even this whole nation. Bring all the tithes into the storehouse, that there may be food in My house, And try Me now in this," Says the LORD of hosts, "If I will not open for you the windows of heaven And pour out for you such blessing That there will not be room enough to receive it. Malachi 3:8-10*

Now, you will be pleased to know I am not going to get into a theological debate about tithing, whether it is Old or New Testament, whether it applies today, or whether Jesus taught about it - which He did:

"But woe to you Pharisees! For you tithe mint and rue and all manner of herbs, and pass by justice and the love of God. These you ought to have done, without leaving the others undone. Luke 11:42*

This is just Jean and my story about our experience in tithing. All I know is that tithing blesses us, it blesses the churches we have been in and it is in the Bible. Jumble sales, cream teas, quiz nights, bingo and so on, are not in the Bible, and certainly not as ways of providing for God's house. Sorry, I said I was not getting into that.

So how did we get into tithing? Well, "we" is probably not the right place to start, I was earning really good money when we became Christians, and I was pretty much ignoring any mention of tithing (giving 10%). Jean, however, kept coming across it in teaching she was hearing and in her Bible reading. (Gentlemen, if you are a bit tight then it would probably be best to get your wife a New Testament, and keep her away from the Old Testament, or at least rip out the book of Malachi, however I would warn you that you will only be cheating yourself.) God can manage well enough without your money, but can you manage without God's blessing? Maybe you think you can, but you will never know the up-side of tithing until you try it, and not just for a week or so but as a lifestyle. God's promises are Yes and Amen.

For all the promises of God in Him are Yes, and in Him Amen, to the glory of God through us. 2 Corinthians 1:20

And what a promise this is, "'try Me now in this,' Says the Lord of hosts, 'If I will not open for you the windows of heaven and pour out for you such blessing That there will not be room enough to receive it.'" (Malachi 3:10). Jean and I were fairly new Christians (probably about six months or so), Jean was on fire and I was just getting kindled up, so to speak, but we were now attending a church and the giving side of being a Christian came up, as in the money giving side of being a Christian came up, and as we were now attending a church it became unavoidable. So, it happened, one day while living in France and as I said, still fairly new Christians, we decided to tithe, (I think Jean had the casting vote, but I must say with all honesty I have never regretted it).

Sitting in our kitchen I got out my payslips and bank statements and calculator and started to work out what this was going to mean in real money. As I sat there, Jean said 'What's so hard?' I started to explain to her that I was paid some of my salary in Francs directly into my French bank account at a set exchange rate, and that the money I had paid into my UK bank account I transferred out at a variable rate. After watching me for some time she came over from the cooker and said 'What's so hard? Just move the point from there to there'. I never realised she had suddenly become a maths expert. We agreed on the figure and had it paid into the bank account of the church we were then attending, 'The English Speaking Church of Toulouse' an Anglican congregation who met in the Catholic Church in Pibrac. That was the next thing, we were now paying our tithes but was paying the tithe into this small church, right? After all they didn't have a building, they didn't really have any expenses, I bet nobody else is tithing, what are they going to do with my money? At this point I felt God say to me, you are only responsible to give the tithe, what they do with your tithe is between them and Me. I have found that very freeing, wherever we have been going to church since then we have been tithing to that church and how they handle that tithe is between them and God, after all it is all God's money anyway, and we get to keep 90%.

We have tithed now for 20 years, we also give regularly on top of that, but no matter what position we have been in we have tithed 10% of our income, from when I had a large salary in France to when we were both unemployed. Whether we were on part time wages or, as now, on a salary (all be it a fraction of what I earned 20 years ago) we have been faithful to tithe and God has been faithful in blessing us, God has always provided for our needs and so often above and beyond anything we could have imagined, some of which stories are in this book (particularly our daughter's wedding). So, try God, (He says to try Him, not me) and see what blessings flow.

Oh, taste and see that the Lord is good; Blessed is the man who trusts in Him! Psalm 34:8

And remember....

Each of you should give what you have decided in your heart to give, not reluctantly or under compulsion, for God loves a cheerful giver.
2 Corinthians 9:7 (NIVUK)

8

Saint Germaine

but whoever drinks of the water that I shall give him will never thirst. But the water that I shall give him will become in him a fountain of water springing up into everlasting life." John 4:14

It was 1998 and two years since we had moved with my job to a small village in France with our daughter Kerry. It was a world away from the small village in Scotland where we had come from, but not a world away from our problems. We had always been drinkers but now it had come to a head. Jean gave her heart to Jesus, kneeling in front of a TV screen, not knowing what she was doing or what it all meant. I thought she had gone mad, but our lives were to change forever.

Jean awoke one dark November night to see her standing by our bed, a young girl with long blonde hair, just standing there. She waited on her to speak but she never did. Jean soon fell back asleep but when she awoke in the morning, she could remember her vividly. She told me about what she had seen, who could she be? She thought she had seen a ghost, but had had no feeling of fear or anxiety even though, up to this point, her life had been full of fear. Jean sensed she meant her no harm only good but what it all meant she had no idea.

Not long after that Jean started having trouble with her stomach it was diagnosed as gall stones, but also added to this she had stomach ulcers which they were going to have to treat before they would attempt an operation to remove her gall bladder. While living in France the years of heavy drinking had taken their toll and the effects were all too obvious in her stomach complaint, but Jean did not want to be treated in a foreign country. The thought of having to speak to French doctors and be in a French hospital was her worst nightmare.

We were working through problems in our marriage, and we had been guided to a woodland walk at the edge of our village 'Chemin des Anes' (the way of donkeys), where we used to walk round thrashing out our problems. One day when Jean was walking alone, she walked a little further than normal and came across a small grotto with a constant stream of water. It was rather over-grown, but the water was fresh and clear. Jean felt Jesus was telling her to take a drink from the spring each day as she passed by and believe Him for her healing. As a new Christian all this was strange to her, but she felt compelled to trust Jesus, so each day as she passed by the grotto she would go in through the small archway and take a drink from the spring, thanking and believing Jesus for her healing. This went on for several months, Jean knew she was getting better; the discomfort in her stomach was easing.

Then one fine French spring day Jean went to the grotto as usual, she took her usual drink from the spring and thanked Jesus for her healing. As she turned to walk away, she realised that someone had been and tidied up the grotto. The bushes and trees all around were cut back and as she looked at the grotto, she saw something she had never noticed before. On top of the grotto where the bushes had all been cut back there was now a statue visible. The statue was of a young girl with a lamb at her feet. She was dressed in old fashioned clothing and wearing a white linen scarf over her head and it looked like she had long blonde hair, she was the girl in Jean's bedroom. There could be no mistake; it had not been a ghost after all, but an angelic vision.

When Jean shared her story with our pastor and his wife, they told her that the grotto was called "la fontaine Sainte-Germaine" and that the statue was that of Sainte Germaine, a young shepherd girl and the patron saint for rural girls; many healing miracles had been attributed to her. Jesus had used a vision of Sainte Germaine to speak to Jean, the lost sheep, who with her young faith and steadfast obedience was healed.

Jean was a new Christian and was embarrassed about thinking this vision from God had been a ghost, but then the Lord took her to Matthew 14v26 where the disciples, on seeing Jesus walking on the water, cried out "It is a ghost!"

He was reassuring her that we do not always understand what He is doing or what is happening around us, but when we are patient and faithful to God's prompting all will be revealed. It was the start of an amazing journey with Jesus which continues to this day, where we have seen more miracles of healing, provision and above all God's grace. We returned to the United Kingdom at the end of 2000, alcohol free, healed and set free to a new life in Christ Jesus.

Therefore if the Son makes you free, you shall be free indeed.
John 8:36

9

Bible College. God's Provision

*And my God shall supply all your need according to His riches in glory
by Christ Jesus.* Philippians 4:19

I was now a fully committed Christian, whatever that meant I had no
idea, so I thought I better go and find out.

Whilst watching the God Channel, I got to hear of Colin Urquhart and
Kingdom Faith Bible College and believed God was calling me there.
With a little encouragement from Jean, I applied. My wife is a great one
for chapping doors, if you think you have a prompting from God, then
chap some doors, believing that God is big enough to open a door than
no one can shut.

"See, I have placed before you an open door that no one can shut."
Revelation 3:18 (NIVUK)

She also believes that He can shut doors that no one can open. It works
for us and I recommend you try it and see what adventures God has for
you. I was accepted for Bible college, despite not having been able to
attend for a face to face interview which was the normal practice for
this Bible college. We were still living in France at the time, and it was
quite impractical to fly over 1,000 miles for an interview. My
application and letter from my current minister were deemed
sufficient, so I was off to Bible college. Only I was still employed, my
wife was not, and we had a thirteen year old daughter attending school
in France.

France had been a big step up for me work wise. I was earning good
money, getting good resettling allowances and now, after seventeen

years with the same reputable company, British Aerospace, I was going to pack it all in, just like that. Found Jesus, lost the plot?

At this time, as often is the case in the Aerospace industry, there was a redundancy going around. So, I thought that's it, God's provision, I applied for my redundancy. I got the letter through with my estimated pay out, £19,500 pounds. Enough to see my way back to the UK and get established. In reality, it was less than six months wages and wasn't going to last that long but it was certainly a boost to our faith walk, God was providing. Then it happened, my manager called me in to discuss my application for redundancy and told me I wasn't eligible. If I left the company, he would have to replace me, therefore my job wasn't redundant, therefore I couldn't be made redundant. I said that I would be leaving anyway.

"Now faith is confidence in what we hope for and assurance about what we do not see." Hebrews 11:1 (NIV)

Our Faith was going to be really tested now, and worse was to come. I received a phone call from the finance department in British Aerospace, Woodford, where my salary was paid from. The gentleman said to me 'You realise you have resigned?' I said yes, he then went on to tell me that I would have to make my own way back to the United Kingdom from France, I would be responsible for all my removal costs and flights for myself and my family, there was no way they could pay anything as it would set a precedent, meaning anyone could just resign and insist British Aerospace resettle them back to the United Kingdom. I said, 'That's fine, I understand, trying to keep cool and grounded in my newfound faith. I told Jean, she said 'That's ok, God is our provider now, not British Aerospace'.

We made preparations to leave France. We put the house on the market, the estate agent said we weren't asking enough, they could get us more, and that in France all the fees are paid by the buyer, praise God. We put the house on the market in August, I was due to start Bible college in September, but Jean and Kerry would not be moving back to England till December. I am not quite sure how we came up with this arrangement as it meant Jean and Kerry would be in France for up to four months with no income and a mortgage still to pay. We were told it usually takes about six months to sell a house, so we thought we better get the house on the market. The first person who came to see it bought it at the asking price and agreed to wait till December to move in, that's my God.

Shortly after that I got a phone call from ATIC, the office that helped with settling in and repatriation. They said I still had a couple of free flights to use, did I want to use them? I said I would like Jean and Kerry to be able to come and see me at Bible college at half term but that I would have left the company by then, she said if you book them before you leave the company that will be alright, definitely God's favour. Things were starting to turn around.

Next, they phoned to see if I had made any arrangements for moving our furniture back to the UK, I said I hadn't, they asked if they could send someone round for estimates. The upshot was that they ended up paying for all our furniture to be shipped back to the UK and stored for 6 weeks while we arranged a rented house; this wasn't British Aerospace this was God, and that wasn't the end of it. They then asked when we would be flying back to the UK as a family and booked flights for us to fly back in December, and that still wasn't the end of it, when we got on the plane we were in first class, and why not? We serve a first-class God.

The whole situation turned round from not able to do anything to paying for everything. Whilst I didn't get my redundancy from British Aerospace, God made sure that I was not out of pocket in following His call. This was how it was going to be for us from now on, our faith had to be in the unseen provision of God and not in salaries or wage packets. It would be fifteen years before I would be in regular full-time employment again, and even then, fifteen years later, my wages would be 50% less, but God would keep us provided for in many different ways. Providing not for our wants, but our needs, and sometimes we needed to get what we wanted, and God provided there too.

We spent two years at Bible college, I did two years and Jean did the first year, it was an amazing jump start to our faith walk, something that I desperately needed. I tried to run after the first year, but God called me to do the second year, and this meant that Jean could do the first year. We were living in an expensive area of West Sussex, renting a beautiful house and being blessed by the Lord. During the summer months I decided I needed to get some work and went to the local Job Centre. After taking all my details the woman said I don't think you will be eligible for any benefits, I said I wasn't looking for benefits I was looking for work, she still insisted on me going through the application for benefits that she said I wouldn't get. I ended up walking out, went down the street and walked into a local employment agency. I started the next day doing practically a different job every other week, kitchen porter, van driver, factory worker, envelope filler, doing it all unto the Lord, and He was faithful, I never had a day without work the entire summer.

Can God Talk Through a Lawnmower?

Then the LORD opened the mouth of the donkey, and she said to Balaam, "What have I done to you, that you have struck me these three times?" Numbers 22:28

It was the summer of 2000 and I was getting ready to go to Kingdom Faith Bible College in Horsham in West Sussex. We were still living in France at the time and for some strange reason I was going to Bible college to start in September and Jean and Kerry weren't due to come back to the UK until the December school holidays. This puzzled me. Throughout our now 18 years of marriage Jean and I had never been separated other than the two spells she had in hospital. First, when she had our daughter Kerry and spent some time convalescing at Thorneyflat Hospital after a particularly difficult forceps delivery, and secondly two months later when she had a heart attack at the age of 24. Both necessary and both beyond our control. But now, we had made a decision which meant I would spend the first term at Bible college, ten weeks, on my own in England while Jean and Kerry stayed in France. I was not sure what this was all about and that is when it happened.

I was cutting the grass at our home in Pibrac and asking God why I was going back to the UK on my own. I felt the Lord was saying to me that if this lawnmower broke down, I would have to take it apart to fix it and then put it back together again properly. This was what He was doing with Jean and I, He was taking us apart so He could fix us and then bring us back together properly. I shared this with Jean, she was excited that I had heard from God.

Now whether you believe God speaks to us today or not, I was convinced that what I got was from God and it was enough to settle my mind and give me peace to do what I believed God was calling me to do, in the way that God wanted me to do it and in His timing. I was going to Bible college on my own at the age of 41, having been married for 18 years.

I was actually quite relieved to be going to England, at least there they spoke English. That is when I discovered God had a sense of humour, I ended up sharing a small room, with bunk beds and one chair (it wasn't big enough to give us a chair each) with Dominic, a young man from Switzerland who spoke German, and wasn't too great understanding a broad Scottish accent, although he did speak English.

Bible college was a whole new experience to me not just the spiritual but the practical. I went from a detached villa with a swimming pool in southwest France to sharing a box room with a stranger, worse was to come. When we arrived, we were allocated our rooms. There was a men's corridor, a lady's corridor and a married couple's corridor. Being there on my own I was in the men's corridor. The housekeeping rotas were up for our corridor and as I checked them, I found to my relief I wasn't on the toilet cleaning rota that would be a bit much, you can't expect a married man to clean toilets, right? Wrong!

The first Wednesday after lunch we met to be allocated our house keeping duties. Each Wednesday for the next ten weeks we would be involved in doing housekeeping in and around the college. As I sat there the list of duties were being read out and volunteers required for each, it came to toilet cleaning, the young man next to me, shot up his arm and, much to my surprise, so did my arm. I had just volunteered to clean toilets. Not just in our corridor, but in all three corridors, and not just the toilets but the showers and the baths as well. Jonathan, wherever you are, I forgive you. I went on to do a summer placement with that young man. As I said, "God has a sense of humour".

Kingdom Faith

And do not be conformed to this world, but be transformed by the renewing of your mind, that you may prove what is that good and acceptable and perfect will of God. Romans 12:2

I was now a Christian, but what that meant I was not sure. I knew things had to change, steeped in sin and a self-centred lifestyle and surrounded by people of the same mind-sets I was unlikely to change by staying where I was. I had put my faith in me and what I could do (earn) for long enough, it was time to put my faith in God and totally rely on Him. But what did that mean, what did a 'committed' Christian do? What was expected of you by God and by those around you?

I was working a shift pattern which included Sunday working, and despite it being illegal in France I worked seven days a week. When we arrived in France our department were required to provide cover for our customers seven days a week, 24 hours a day, we had a limited number of staff to do this with. We needed a shift pattern which covered this without going outwith the French Employment laws which banned working seven days a week and excessive overtime. I came up with a shift system that enabled us to work seven days in a row, 5 from one week and 2 from the next week; the shift pattern involved 12-hour days and a lot of time off and everybody was happy with this. That was then, this is now, and I am a Christian, who does not work seven days in a row (no matter which week they are in) and is looking to be of on the Sunday to be with other worshipping Christians. I asked for Sundays off and was told, no problem, you just have to get someone to cover for you. It was a complicated shift pattern which meant swapping was very difficult without ruining someone else's time off, and besides the Sabbath (i.e. Sunday) is held as sacred to the Saturday night party animal as it is to the Sunday morning church goer, possibly even more so, unfortunately. Their Sunday morning day of rest (and recovery) is paramount to having a 'good' Saturday night. As expected, I could never get a swap.

This led me to looking at other aspects of my life and how things were going to change if I was going to become a new creation in Christ Jesus. I needed to be 'transformed by the renewing of my mind'. We were watching Christian TV to get most of our teaching and after six months had ended up at church, 'The English Speaking Church of Toulouse.' During this time, I had been watching Pastor Colin Urquhart from Kingdom Faith Ministries and on one of his programmes I saw an advert for their Bible college and immediately felt God was speaking to me to go there. It was going to be a huge sacrifice and life would never be the same, no matter what the outcome of my time there should be. I would be giving up a good steady (large) income, we would have to sell the house and there would be no guarantee of an income at the end of it, but the renewing of my mind and the transforming of my lifestyle was paramount to keeping what was important to me, my wife Jean and my daughter Kerry. I could not go on the way I was and expect to keep a relationship alive, I needed a complete fresh start, which Christ was offering me, but because of the years of living 'my way' I needed a jump start in living God's way. In September 2000 I left my job and took my family back to England to start a really new life, in Christ. Despite never having a full-time job again until March 2014, I can honestly say I have no regrets and that God has been faithful in providing much more than I ever did, not financially, but in so many other ways that bring peace and stability in times of hardship. We have never been in desperate need financially, well to the world we have, but our view on financial needs is so different now. God has always pulled us through and, looking back, these have been some of the most blessed times in our walk with God, just to see His hand in our everyday lives first-hand and to know He is with us always.

I had planned to just do one year at Kingdom Faith Bible College but ended up staying (kicking and screaming) for two. They were two blessed years, although being in West Sussex the cost of living took every last penny of our savings, meaning relying on God even more. The first year was indeed a kick start to my Faith learning the disciplines of Bible study, praying and putting God first in everything I do. The habit (not all habits are bad) of giving God the first part of your day has been a mainstay of my Christian walk and one which I continue today. Anytime that I don't spend quality time with God but just a quick hello and a muffled prayer before I leave the house, it always shows up later in the day in my attitudes and lack of 'Spiritual Fruit' (Galatians 5 v 22 - 23). It was the jump start I needed and while at times I do not necessarily see any direct outcome of my two years there, it set me apart from the world and helped me make the break I was looking for from my past. There was a definite season of going from the kingdom of darkness into the Kingdom of Light and the help and direction I received in doing this while at Bible college I will be eternally grateful for.

I came out of there with my wife Jean and daughter Kerry and headed off into the big bad world, little did I realise that some of that big bad world we would find in the church, but that is another story. We were renewed, refreshed and better prepared for not only life in the world but life as a Christian family. Challenges were ahead but our foundation in Christ had been laid.

Baptism

He who believes and is baptized will be saved; but he who does not believe will be condemned. Mark 16:16

In December 2000, after three months at Bible college I was baptised. I did not realise at the time that in the denominational churches like the Church of Scotland where I was baptised as a baby and the Church of England, where I am now that this was not the 'done thing'. If I had been baptised as a baby then that was it once and for all, I could not be baptised again.

one Lord, one faith, one baptism. Ephesians 4:5

Now it quite clearly states one baptism, but it does not say baptised once. I was baptised after my first birth and now having been born again I wanted to be baptised after my new birth in Christ Jesus. While totally ignorant of the controversial nature of my adult baptism, after having been baptised as a baby, I was fully aware of the compulsion I had to be baptised. The verse above in Mark, says, 'those who believe and are baptised will be saved'. I now believed and I wanted to be baptised as a public acknowledgement of my newfound faith in Christ. I certainly could not claim to have believed at a few months old so how could I be baptised into anything but my parents' faith. Interestingly, all through my life I was never aware that I had been baptised, I knew I had been christened as a baby, and in fact we had our daughter christened when she was a baby, but I never related it to baptism. Now there are those who will say that the words 'I baptise you in the name of the Father and of the Son and of the Holy Spirit' should have been a bit of a clue but I can honestly say they were not. It was a ritual that you put your child through, then had a party. Now I know there are people who are very sincere when they present their child for baptism and I am not knocking that, but there are many like ourselves who just do it because it's what you do. There are also those who believe that you have to be baptised to get into heaven and therefore they want their child baptised in case the worst happens.

While the above verse talks about being baptised to be saved it also talks about belief and unbelief and until we can get to the stage where we are capable of making that distinction and that choice for ourselves then God will not condemn us, and therefore, as I see it, being baptised requires us to also get to the stage where we can have our own faith and not our parents faith. I believed so firmly that I was to be baptised that I was baptised while my wife Jean and daughter Kerry were still in France. It was the end of term at Bible college and they were having a baptismal service in the Bible college itself, which hadn't been done for years. There was a baptismal tank under the stage in the worship hall, they cleared the stage of instruments and filled the tank (with cold water) and I, an Italian man, an English man and a woman from Pakistan were baptised in front of 60 or 70 Bible college students and pastors. It was an amazing feeling coming up out of that water and one you never forget. I would recommend it to everyone. Dead to sin and self and alive in Christ, Alleluia.

When Jean and Kerry came over to join me at Bible college they too would be baptised by full immersion as adults making their own choice to stand for Christ. That was a great night, they had a slightly larger audience, around six or seven hundred at Kingdom Faith Church in Horsham, and in the congregation that night were Jean's mum and dad who just happened to be visiting us from Scotland when she was getting baptised. We were never quite sure what they made of it, being Church of Scotland, Jean's dad being an elder, and all the tradition and straight-lacedness that involved. Now here they were in a warehouse full of people worshipping and praising God at the top of their voices and Jean and Kerry being baptised in a tank of water, not quite what they were used to but God had them there at that time for a reason.

We were all now as a family baptised into Christ, the old had gone and the new was and still is with us, thank you Jesus.

England

and said to him, 'Get out of your country and from your relatives, and come to a land that I will show you.' Acts 7:3

until I come and take you away to a land like your own land, a land of grain and new wine, a land of bread and vineyards. Isaiah 36:17

Having felt the call of God to go to Bible college and believing that Bible college to be Kingdom Faith under Colin Urquhart we ended up in England. Now, coming from Scotland we were definitely coming out of our country and away from our relatives, but we had already done that when we moved to France. When I left Scotland for France, I said I would never be back in Scotland, that was before I became a Christian when my choices (mostly bad) were my own. I was to learn that you never say never to God, and that one day I would be back in Scotland living, but that is another chapter, for the time being we were going to England and, being Scottish, I had never thought of England as the 'Promised Land'. The land was now definitely like my own land, they spoke the same language, and it was indeed to prove a land where God would provide for us in so many ways.

When we landed back in the United Kingdom, we spent some time in Scotland over the Christmas holidays before heading back for the next term at Bible college and England. We did not have a car and we were going to need one, we had given our Ford Mondeo to our pastor prior to leaving France and were now in the UK with no car. We reckoned on a budget of £2,000 to buy a car and one day as we were driving past a garage, we saw a Volvo sitting outside with a price tag of £2,500, we liked the look of it, went in to see about it and decided to buy it. I said to Jean but it's more than our budget, she said it's our car and our budget is £2,000 so give him £2,000 for it. I went in and seen the salesman and offered him £2,000, he said 'well I'm not exactly busy at this time of the year, you can have it for £2,000', Praise God, it was a great car lasting us several years and many miles, including a trip to France to pick up our dog.

Heading off to England as a family just seemed so natural and we spent several years there, first at Bible college and then as part of a church plant. We had the issue of finding Kerry a school in Horsham and as we were to find out again and again God would provide the best. In Horsham Kerry ended up at Millais School, one of the best in the area at the time and today it is still classed as an 'outstanding school'. The only thing was that it was an all-girls school, Kerry was not happy. I think she thought we were sending her to some sort of private school or boarding school, we were not used to single sex schools where we came from, however she quickly settled in and excelled. When it came time to move on, we were heading to Lincolnshire to a small market town called Alford. Again, we had the issue of finding Kerry a school and once again God provided the best. This time it was Queen Elizabeth Grammar school, and once again Kerry wasn't sure what type of school we were sending her to, 'grammar school' was another term we were unfamiliar with in Scotland. It is also called a 'selective school' which meant Kerry had to pass a test before being admitted, which she did with flying colours. Kerry has always proved resilient and adaptable, she settled in and, being the girl she is, made new friends and left for university with straight A's.

Kerry and her husband Andrew now have their own children, one of whom, Rufus, has just become old enough for primary school; they are taking him from the local pre-school where he has made friends and putting him in the 'best' school in the next village. We don't have a leg to stand on when it comes to saying 'maybe you should leave him where he is.' But God provided the best schools for our daughter and now He is just providing the best schools for our grandson. We were to spend two years in Horsham and then another four years in Lincolnshire before returning to Scotland for eight years and then God brought us back to 'the promised land' England. I have now discovered that God's Promised Land is wherever He calls you to for that season and not just where I would like to be.

Blessings on Obedience.......

"Now it shall come to pass, if you diligently obey the voice of the Lord your God, to observe carefully all His commandments which I command you today, that the Lord your God will set you high above all nations of the earth. And all these blessings shall come upon you and overtake you, because you obey the voice of the Lord your God: "Blessed shall you be in the city, and blessed shall you be in the country. Deuteronomy 28 1-3

For the time being that city is Liverpool, and the country is England, and we continue to be blessed as we serve God together. Amen.

A Chipped Dog

The LORD is good to all, And His tender mercies are over all His works.
Psalm 145:9

When it came time to leave France, we had a problem in our dog Hazel; she was 12 years old and there was no way we were going to bring her into the UK and leave her in kennels for six months in quarantine. The quarantine laws stated that animals brought into the UK had to be quarantined for six months. We were not prepared to do this, so what was our option? As we made enquiries, we discovered that that very year (2000), the laws had been changed. God is so good. This meant that dogs and cats traveling with their owners from most European countries would be able to enter the UK without having to spend six months in quarantine. We were so relieved and blessed by this change which we had no idea was happening; God was working in the background long before we even knew we would be returning to the UK. In order to qualify for exemption from quarantine a dog had to be microchipped with an ISO Standard microchip and vaccinated against rabies with an approved inactivated adjuvanted vaccine. Once a successful blood test had been achieved, the owner would be given a certificate for their pet, containing the microchip number and the vaccination and blood test details, signed by a qualified veterinary surgeon. We contacted our local vet who was able to do this, and Hazel now had a passport to travel to the UK.

We flew back to the UK in December 2000 and in January we drove back to France to collect our dog. We were living in temporary accommodation prior to moving into a rented house and the man whose house we were sharing heard what we were doing and said to us that he had a voucher for the Euro Tunnel we could have. By this time we had no income and were living by faith, so, praise God, we booked our car on the train and travelled free under the Channel and back. Sometimes we overlook the small details in our stories: the big detail, having the law changed just months before our return to the UK, we readily remember, but sometimes we forget the little details, living in a house in Horsham, West Sussex, the other side of London from Folkestone and the Euro Tunnel, and the guy whose house we were sharing just happened to have a ticket for the Euro Tunnel going spare. God is so good and interested in every area of our lives, even our dogs.

And my God will meet all your needs according to the riches of his glory in Christ Jesus. Philippians 4:19 (NIV)

Not just all our big needs and asks, but all our needs, no matter how insignificant they may appear to us: God is listening.

I Can Do All Things....

I can do all things through Christ who strengthens me.
Philippians 4:13

Some people critique Christianity as being a 'crutch.' Crutches are usually something you lean on while the body is healing itself and the aim is to one day discard them and be back to being yourself. Christianity as prescribed in the Bible, is not a short-term fix and it definitely does not leave you to heal yourself, but through a relationship with Jesus Christ, guides you and supports you through all of life's ups and downs. Most of us, whether we like to admit it or not, will lean on something or someone at different points in our lives. For some it becomes the main thing in their life and what gets them through every day. For others for different seasons, they use different 'crutches', just like we need different crutches or splints to help our bodies heal. But that leaves us to search for different things at different times whereas Jesus is a constant that never changes.

Jesus Christ is the same yesterday, today, and forever. Hebrews 13:8

And He promises to be there for us always.

".... and lo, I am with you always, even to the end of the age." Amen.
Matthew 28:20

Even depending on our self can become a crutch, our own self-sufficiency leading us to be leaning on something which we believe to be safe but can crumble at any time. Jesus is not a crutch, He is a rock, someone we can depend on, someone whom, if we build our lives on, will be there for us and who will see us through the bad times as well as the good. We don't have to wait until the storms come and then try and build on the rock as most of us (including me) do, it is much easier and safer to build during the calm seasons in our life. But the good news is even if you have waited until the storms of life are overwhelming you it is never too late to build upon the rock. Jesus will give you the strength to build in the storms of life and having done so to stand.

"Therefore whoever hears these sayings of Mine (Jesus's), and does them, I will liken him to a wise man who built his house on the rock: and the rain descended, the floods came, and the winds blew and beat on that house; and it did not fall, for it was founded on the rock. Matthew 7:24-25

When I graduated from Bible college, I was asked to give my testimony on life at Bible college and how I ended up there. I started by saying 'Before I became a Christian, I didn't need God, I was God. I could do all things through 'drink' which strengthened me.' It got a laugh, but it was not funny, it was pathetic, pathetic because it was true. But being my own self-sufficient God (good job, lots of money) and relying on drink to see me through, had caused a potentially great marriage to be one of despair and desperation on the brink of divorce. Thinking everything is alright led me to ignore the real situations around me and left the important things in life, my wife Jean and my daughter Kerry, as mere bit parts in my oh so important life. Sad, sick and empty, using drink to keep up appearances, until it happened: life caught up with me, as it always does, and I was in for a dose of reality. It came through Jean coming to Jesus and challenging me to really look at my life and it really hurt. When you spend your life thinking you are a 'nice guy', the truth hurts. But only the truth will set you free, and only standing on the rock, the truth that is Jesus, will get you through the other side. Once I accepted that truth Jesus could help and He did, we got to the place where we now actually have that great marriage and my daughter, her husband and our two grandsons are the icing on the cake. Things that I would not be a part of if I had kept on in 'my way'. I am forever grateful I chose His way, and that Jesus has been with me every step of the way. Jesus is 'the way'.

Jesus said to him, "I am the way, the truth, and the life. No one comes to the Father except through Me. John 14:6

Jesus is the truth.

Then Jesus said to those Jews who believed Him, "If you abide in My word, you are My disciples indeed. And you shall know the truth, and the truth shall make you free." They answered Him, "We are Abraham's descendants, and have never been in bondage to anyone. How can You say, 'You will be made free'?" Jesus answered them, "Most assuredly, I say to you, whoever commits sin is a slave of sin. And a slave does not abide in the house forever, but a son abides forever. Therefore if the Son makes you free, you shall be free indeed.
John 8:31-36

And Jesus is the life.

".... I have come that they may have life, and that they may have it more abundantly." John 10:10

Suicide Is Not Painless

Then he threw down the pieces of silver in the temple and departed, and went and hanged himself. Matthew 27:5

There are several examples of suicide in the Bible: Samson, Saul and as quoted above, Judas, to name but a few. The main characteristics being that of hopelessness: Samson saw no way out of his predicament, blinded and imprisoned by the Philistines, Saul was gravely injured and wanted to avoid being captured by his enemies and Judas felt what he had done could not be undone and therefore could not be forgiven. Whatever the circumstances, suicide generally comes from feeling hopeless and that everybody would be 'better off without me.' Neither of which is true. There is a God of hope and no one is better off with the thought that, 'if only I had... said this, done that, listened more, seen it coming...' Suicide can destroy the lives of those who you think are 'better off without you.' Those of us of a certain age may remember the theme tune to MASH, a programme set in a field hospital in Vietnam during the American – Vietnam war. It had the striking lines, 'suicide is painless, It brings on many changes, And I can take or leave it if I please' nothing could be further from the truth.

When we first became Christians in France, we left everything and went to Bible college. All hell seemed to break loose. While at Bible college Jean's dad had a severe stroke, we left Bible college and went up to Scotland where we stayed for six weeks as the family adjusted to their new circumstances. While we were staying in Scotland and staying with Jean's parents, we received a phone call from Bobby her younger brother. He was in Calais in France waiting on a ferry; he was a long-distance lorry driver and the phone call was quite disturbing as he was really paranoid about people being smuggled on board his truck, even to the point where he accused me of being 'in on it'. However, he made it back to Dover and his home base of Castle Douglas where he left his lorry, and his job, and phoned me to pick him up. During the drive back, he spoke of suicide and how he was going to see his son's first Christmas and then end it all. Christmas was a couple of months away and therefore you would think there would have been plenty of time to talk to him about it. The next morning, I awoke and said to Jean we need to pray for Bobby; a little while later the police arrived at Jean's parents' home to tell them that Bobby had been found in a car with a hosepipe in it, he was alive. Praise God. He had been found in an isolated woodland spot by some workmen who were renovating a nearby farmhouse and just happened to see his car and went to investigate. Prayer is powerful. There are not many farms in the area, or in Scotland for that matter, with Biblical names but the farm where he was found was called Pisgah, an extremely unusual name for a farm but a sign that God had his hand in Bobby's life. But what was Bobby going to do with it?

Then Moses went up from the plains of Moab to Mount Nebo, to the top of Pisgah, which is across from Jericho. And the Lord showed him all the land of Gilead as far as Dan, Deuteronomy 34:1

Bobby was admitted to the nearby psychiatric hospital and whilst there Jean tried to talk to him about Jesus, gave him a Bible and talked to him about truth. He asked, what is truth? Jean replied that Jesus is the truth. Bobby had unconfessed sin in his life, which he confessed, but confessing sin isn't enough unless you can accept forgiveness, which God gives freely, but man can withhold to punish you. Unless we know that God's forgiveness is enough and that man may not always get around to forgiving us, then we can get into a never-ending cycle of trying to win back the approval of those we have hurt, people who when they are hurting the most will fling it back in your face. Hurting people hurt people, and without Jesus in the relationship it can become a seemingly hopeless cycle with no end in sight. Is that what happened to Bobby? We will never know, all we know is that in two years' time he would try it again, and this time succeed.

We were living in Sutton-on-Sea at the time, Jean was helping out at a charity shop, running it for the elderly lady who was in the hospital. I dropped in to see her and she was feeling very ill at ease, something was stirring in her spirit. She shut the charity shop at lunch time and went home, still at unease she began praying in tongues and crying out to Jesus. By evening she was still unsettled in her spirit so when Kerry came home from school instead of cooking, we went out for a Chinese meal to Mablethorpe. We returned home and that was when we received the phone call, Bobby had committed suicide and this time he was 'successful'. At the age of thirty-three he was dead. It is still hard to write those words all these years later: suicide is not painless. Jean has many unanswered questions, and the 'Did I do enough?', 'Did I say enough?', Was I there enough?' all came up and will remain unanswered mostly because there is no answer to these questions. But the one question Jean did get an answer to was when Jean asked God 'Where is Bobby now? Is he with You?' On the drive up to Scotland, Jean got a word from the Lord,

For He says to Moses, "I will have mercy on whomever I will have mercy, and I will have compassion on whomever I will have compassion." Romans 9:15

Jean's question arose from something in the back of her mind that said that if you committed suicide then you died in sin, it was self-murder. This is a belief or a teaching or something like that that some people still hold to, but God was saying it was up to Him. A compassionate God would not commit to Hell someone who obviously was out of their mind at the time. Something had snapped, an action was taken which could not be taken back, but it could be forgiven by a loving and caring God, our God, the God of hope. Then in a vision or a dream or whatever it was we don't know, but we do know it was God, Jean saw Bobby at the time of his death. He was looking at someone and when he asked 'Who are you?', that someone said 'I'm Jesus' to which Bobby replied 'Oor Jean was telling the truth.' Bobby had a huge smile on his face, it was the exact time Jean was travailing in the Spirit and crying out in tongues. Bobby had the truth, and he was going to the Father.

Jesus said to him, "I am the way, the truth, and the life. No one comes to the Father except through Me. John 14:6

We went to see Bobby at the funeral parlour at the insistence of Jean's father, we were concerned what Bobby would look like after such a horrific death; he had hanged himself. When we saw him in the coffin, he had a huge smile on his face and Jean said that's how he looked in the vision. She mentioned to his partner about it, she had found him, and she said that is what he looked like when she found him. Jesus had taken him home and he now had the peace that, for whatever reason, he could not find on this earth.

and the peace of God, which surpasses all understanding, will guard your hearts and minds through Christ Jesus. Philippians 4:7

Suicide is not painless; it is not the answer. Those left behind, partners, children, parents, siblings, friends, work colleagues and every other relationship we were in, will all bear some manner of pain and hurt. Many of those relationships that we tell ourselves 'will be better off without us' are the very ones that hurt the most and carry the deepest scars. The statistics on suicide are horrendous, it is not an isolated case here and there, but an epidemic. Many men (and women), without the hope God gives them, have flirted with it. I have. For some, like me, it is a passing moment of frustration and anger at a given situation, for others a half-hearted attempt, a cry for help but for too many others it becomes a reality. 'Suicide remains the leading cause of death in England and Wales for men aged between 20 and 34 years of age (24% of all deaths in 2013) and for men aged 35 to 49 years (13% of all deaths in 2013).' [1]

We must be taking the goodness of the God of hope and His son Jesus Christ to a generation that has lost hope. The song from MASH goes on to say:

'The game of life is hard to play
I'm gonna lose it anyway,
The losing card I'll someday lay
So this is all I have to say, Suicide is painless'

It's a lie from the pit of hell and needs to be exposed for what it is; life is a precious gift and we need to be telling people this and about Jesus who promised us in John 10 v 10 that:

"The thief (Satan) does not come except to steal, and to kill, and to destroy. I (Jesus) have come that they may have life, and that they may have it more abundantly."

1. https://www.ons.gov.uk/peoplepopulationandcommunity/birthsde athsandmarriages/deaths/bulletins/suicidesintheunitedkingdom/20 14-02-18 (accessed 9 June 2021).

Christian Leadership

My brethren, let not many of you become teachers, knowing that we shall receive a stricter judgment. James 3:3

When I left Bible college I felt led to go and be part of a church plant in a small Lincolnshire village. I had been on placement at the planting church in a nearby market town and had visited the church plant where there was no apparent current leadership team. The previous leader was on long term sick leave, in fact one of the first visits I had made when on my placement was to visit him in lying in a darkened room flat on his back with Meniere's disease. This is a disorder of the inner ear that can lead to dizzy spells (vertigo) and hearing loss. He contracted it after an operation on his ear went wrong, he was also a musician and worship leader. Myself and the pastor I was with prayed for him; he did eventually recover to take over the leadership once again but now works for a large American ministry. Jean and I packed up after Bible college and, along with our daughter Kerry, went to be part of the church plant.

Between being interviewed and us arriving at the church they had appointed two 'deacons' who made it quite clear that they had had hands laid on them and that they were in charge. Talk about a deacon-possessed church. One of them came to leadership meetings with his diary to see when he was preaching, then he would promptly put his diary away. The other deacon we had to challenge about her church attendance as it was not setting a good example to the people she was leading. Her answer, 'I don't have to go to church to be a leader in it.' Oh really.

We started the work: God have given me a vision to rebuild the church and while doing it He would rebuild the church. The church was a small run-down building which leaked. The first task was to seal the roof, we were to strip it of slates, put new felt on it and re-slate it. Fortunately, it was a one storey building with a not too sloping roof. At one point whilst on the roof, I took a look around; there was a bank manager, an ex-marine, a businessman, two guys who had served time for attempted murder and myself. God was rebuilding His church. As it happened, God was helping rebuild the building to. One day a small man appeared and asked if we wanted any help; little did we know he was a craftsman and able to help us in every area we would be tackling. He was a Christian from a nearby house church. Praise God.

Things were going well, and I was enjoying bringing the Word on Sundays and just generally doing God's work. We had the church out at our house for a BBQ and for meals. But all was not well. The challenges happened quick and fast. The finger pointing started. Now the reason I haven't given any names or specific locations of the fellowship is because they probably have their own view of things and I don't want to appear to be blaming or saying I was right all the time. No doubt I was not, I was just trying to listen to God and do what He was leading me to do, supported as always by Jean, a source of encouragement and powerful prayer.

We held an Alpha course with amazing success attended completely by men; it was a great source of inspiration. One evening at Alpha, one of the men came in and asked for prayer, he was due in court the next day and he was told it was just a matter of how long he was going away for. He had been found guilty of assault and had a history of violent offences. As he was leaving, I felt the Lord say to me 'He won't do time' I hesitated to tell him, and he was gone out of the door. The next day the news came through, he was not going to jail, and he had been given a suspended sentence. I had missed the opportunity to witness to God, there was no point in saying God had told me after the outcome was known, I had blown it.

Another incident happened when one of our worship team was not going to be able to make it on the Sunday and one of the other worship team members phoned me up to tell me. I had been encouraging him to lead more in the worship. He wanted to bring his brother-in-law in and I said no, it wasn't appropriate and that I had faith he would manage. However, on Sunday when his brother-in-law arrived, he went straight up and grabbed the mike. I asked him to come into the next room where I said he was welcome here as part of the congregation, but it was inappropriate for him to be leading worship. He walked out, along with more than half the church.

Now some people may say I am a bit religious, but I think you have to be aware of who you put up front in church to lead you in worship. This man had just been in found guilty of hitting his daughter from his first relationship whilst being out drunk celebrating the birth of his most recent child to the woman he was now living with. He stated he was not getting married to the girl he had just got pregnant because the pastor in the last church made him get married to the last girl he got pregnant (they were youth leaders in the church at the time) and that marriage hadn't worked. This was his third child to a third woman, and he was proud of himself. He was still living a life of unrepentant sin. I could not condone him representing Christ in such a lifestyle. The relationship between me and his family never really recovered.

After a year there the work on the building was finished and God had confirmed He was in it by supplying every last penny. We had come to work there for a year voluntarily, which we did, and we felt that God was saying it was time to move on. There were lots of small things here and there but the culmination of it all was that they disbanded the leadership team. The lady deacon ended up leaving the area and the male deacon stayed and he continued to get the occasional preaching spot.

Today that small church building is the outreach arm of the church who have moved into a church previously owned by the congregational church. We dropped in on it once but never met anyone we knew; God was doing a new thing but we believe we were part of God's plan to steady the church and be part of the laying of the foundations for what He had planned.

According to the grace of God which was given to me, as a wise master builder I have laid the foundation, and another builds on it. But let each one take heed how he builds on it. 1 Corinthians 3:10

The Real Jesus – Song Number One

He has put a new song in my mouth— Praise to our God; Many will see it and fear, and will trust in the LORD. Psalm 40:3

This song came to me as I drove to a Christian conference in Horsham, West Sussex from our home in Lincolnshire. Conferences are good for Christians, but the world needs to see the real Jesus.

I'm tired of hearing Jesus, and the sick are in their beds
I'm tired of hearing Jesus, and the lame still can't use their legs
I want to see the Real Jesus, I want to see the Real Jesus
The world doesn't need any more religion
It doesn't need another so-called Christian
It needs to see the Real Jesus, I want to see the Real Jesus
I want to see the captives being set free
I want to see the blind people see
I want to see the Real Jesus, I want to see the Real Jesus

19

Driving Route 66. The Story

*Thomas said to Him, "Lord, we do not know where You are going, and
how can we know the way?" Jesus said to him, "I am the way, the
truth, and the life. No one comes to the Father except through Me.*
John 14:5-6

In September 2004 Jean and I had the opportunity to drive Route 66.
We had very little money, but we booked flights and a hire car and
believed God. We were going to drive Route 66 giving out tracts which
we had made up ourselves. 'Route 66, there is only one route through
life: the 66 books of the Bible.' One Route – One Way. Being Scottish I
took my kilt and wore it along the way, the Americans loved it and were
more open to take tracts from us. Two weeks before we were due to
leave, we were given a cheque for £200.00. Praise God we were off.

We planned our route from Los Angeles to Chicago taking in Christian
conferences along the way. In Anaheim we were going to a conference
with Kenneth and Gloria Copeland, then on to Tulsa, Oklahoma where
Jesse Duplantis was due to preach and then Jean was booked in for the
Joyce Meyer Woman's convention in St. Louis, Missouri.

We arrived in Los Angeles and went to pick up our hire car. To save
money we had pre-booked a budget rental, we were told that to pick
up a rental car in Los Angeles and drop it of at Chicago we would be
charged $500, a lot of money. At the desk, the clerk offered us an
upgrade to a van (?) for only $21 a day extra, we said no thanks, he
then offered us it for $14 a day extra, we said no thanks, a budget
would be fine (for driving almost 3000 miles?). He then said we could
have it for $7 a day (less than £4 a day) so we decided to take it. When
we got outside, the van, which is what the Americans call a people

carrier, was a white Dodge Grand Caravan with black tinted windows; we were going in style.

We headed over to Anaheim, home of Disney Land, booked into a small motel with a small pool and praised God. We visited Huntington Beach and Newport Beach. We also went to the conference with Kenneth and Gloria Copeland. Gloria did a healing session. Now I had a problem when I came to having to drive almost 3,000miles. I had forgotten my driving glasses. This was okay for the short term, but when driving long distances on roads I didn't know and trying to keep an eye out for road signs, it was not going to be good. We had never heard of sat-navs back then. I went forward for healing for my eyes and, praise God, my sight improved to the point where driving and looking for direction signs never became a problem over the full 2,750 miles I ended up driving. America is an amazing country, and God's handiwork is shown in creation in so many different landscapes and natural scenery. We started off in California where we could see the vastness and beauty of the Pacific Ocean stretched out before us. We also saw the unpredictability of God's creation as when strolling along Huntington Beach we took our eyes of the sea for a minute only for Jean to be knocked flat by a huge wave. The fact that there were surfers on the beach and that it is a well-known surfing beach should have been a bit of a warning to watch out for waves, but we were only a few feet from the shoreline paddling along and then suddenly. Just like God.

We headed off from California with its sunshine and beaches, through Arizona with more sunshine, so much so that we were driving through desert like landscapes, and on up through New Mexico, Texas, Oklahoma, Kansas, Missouri and Illinois where by now the landscape had become greener and lusher. We ended our journey by resting on Glencoe Beach (how appropriate for a Scottish couple) on the shores of Lake Michigan just outside Chicago. We saw God's guidance and provision and his protection (see Chapter 20) as we spent three weeks living the dream. From His provision of the luxury car at budget prices to His healing of my eyes and to His graciousness throughout the journey in providing accommodation; through God's guidance we ended up at several Hampton Inns, always a warm welcome, a pool and a good breakfast, everything a Pilgrim needs. Although travelling along a very secularly popularised route, we could see God's hand in it and to us it was a time of drawing aside with God, a Pilgrimage.

In all your ways acknowledge Him, And He shall direct your paths.
Proverbs 3:6

We also got our first taste of Christian radio which was amazing and something we would be praying about for the UK when we returned, and, praise God, we now have here in the UK.

Jean even got to attend the Joyce Meyer Women's Conference at the St Louis Dome, not something normally on the Route 66 itinerary, but God ensured that as Jean enabled my desire of driving Route 66 to come to pass, He would enable Jean's desire of being at the Joyce Meyer annual conference to come to pass.

As we headed back to the airport at Chicago, we had one last problem. When we handed the car back, we were due to pay $500 for returning it to Chicago after having picked it up at Los Angeles. We did not have $500. We did however have a credit card, the only reason we had it was because it was a compulsory requirement for car hire in America. We did not want to have to use it and return home $500 in debt. So, we laid hands on the car rental paperwork and believed God that we would not have to pay the $500. In the car rental office, the girl just looked at our paperwork, she had never dealt with someone leaving a car that they had picked up 2,500 miles and six states away. As she sat there, a man appeared from nowhere and said 'Oh I can deal with that', stamped our paperwork and gave us our receipt. We headed out the office double quick and sat in the shuttle bus heading for the airport barely able to look at the paperwork; when we did, we had not been charged the $500, Praise God.

It was the perfect ending to a perfect holiday; God had been in it from day one and was still in it right to the very end.

20

Do You Have a Licence for That?

And Jesus came and spoke to them, saying, "All authority has been given to Me in heaven and on earth." Matthew 28:18

While driving Route 66 we came to St Louis Missouri where Jean would be going to the Joyce Meyer Woman's Conference. I would be giving out tracts in St Louis, as men were not allowed in the conference. Dressed in my kilt and armed with our tracts I headed into St Louis and came across the St Louis Gateway Arch, a prominent landmark in a park down by the river. I promptly settled down to give out our tracts. Sometime later I was approached by a policeman, hand on gun, asking me if 'I had a licence for that?' I had no idea what he meant but it transpired that to give out anything in the park area you needed a licence. I explained I was giving out gospel tracts and that I did not realise that I needed a licence. The officer was very helpful and directed me to City Hall where I could apply for a licence.

A thick Scottish accent, a tartan kilt and God's favour help in these situations, so off I went to City Hall. They required a copy of our tract for their records so, praise God, St Louis City Hall now have a copy of the good news of Jesus Christ in their archives.

The next day I headed back to the St Louis Gateway Arch, standing below it fully licenced and giving out Gospel tracts. After a short while I was approached by an officer, hand hovering over his gun, and said 'Sir, stand away from the crowd'. He obviously did not want to shoot any innocent bystanders. He asked, 'Do you have a licence for that?' Well, this time I did, so I went to reach down into my bag to get it, only for the officer to get a bit excited, 'Stop' he cried. I explained my licence was in the bag, so he let me slowly go into my bag and produce it, after that he said he would radio around and make sure I wasn't disturbed again. Praise God.

I continued to give out tracts until it was time to go and meet up with Jean again. She was in the St Louis dome, worshiping and praising God and sitting under the Word of God, oblivious to the fact that I was almost jailed, or worse shot, for proclaiming Jesus. What a way to go.

The Purple Dyson

And my God shall supply all your needs according to His riches in glory by Christ Jesus. Philippians 4:19

Now when God says He will provide all your needs we can get to thinking house, car, cash, holidays, or perhaps even healing, peace, joy, but a hoover? Well, when it's what you need, it's what you need.

We had just moved from Bible college to Alford in Lincolnshire where we were going to be part of a church plant. God had blessed us with a beautiful cottage in the country, it was part of an old estate. There were cattle grids in the lead up to it, two lakes, woodland and a small chapel all in the grounds of a large mansion now being run as a small private school. It was heaven on earth. The cottage was basic, but we fitted it out as best we could, it had an open fire and we were able to collect fallen trees from the surrounding woodland. We were missing a few household items, but we were a people of faith. When we moved in, the landlord, who ran the school, said that the washing machine in the kitchen didn't work but if we could get it working, we could have it. Our new neighbours, a little way off in another large house, were Christians running a fellowship by the name of Living Waters. Andrew, the leader, dropped in on us and when we told him about the washing machine, he soon had it to bits. There was an internal fuse needing replaced, we bought one for 50p and, praise God, we had a washing machine. We also needed a fridge freezer, one of the students from the Bible college we had come from, was in the nearby town of Louth doing a placement. She and some others came to visit us and she asked about our fridge; it was summer and really needed. We said we were in faith for one, she said she had some money coming later that year and she would buy us one, however we really needed one then and there. A few weeks later, when she was back visiting, we had already been given a fridge freezer, God is good.

We were now lacking one thing, a hoover. We started praying about it and Jean said she would like a Dyson, a purple one. Now these came in at around £200, even if we had that kind of money or were given that much in a blessing, the last thing we would do would be to buy a hoover. Then one day returning from dropping Kerry off at school, I was driving along a country lane leading to our house and saw a hoover box sitting at the side of the road. I stopped and looked, inside it was a Dyson that the owners had put out for the rubbish collection. I put it in the back of the car and headed home. When I got home, I shouted to Jean and she came to see what I had and was amazed to see a Dyson hoover, not just any Dyson, but a purple one. I checked it out, the hose on it was damaged and sucking in air. There was a free phone customer service number on the hoover, I called it and was able to order a new hose for £20. When it arrived, I fitted it and we had a purple Dyson fully working for £20. Praise God who supplies all our needs.

22

Estate Agent / Postman

And whatever you do, do it heartily, as to the Lord and not to men,
Colossians 3:23

While at Alford Christian Centre it came time for me to get a job. Terry, one of the Deacons, was a Chartered Surveyor and ran his own estate agency. He had decided to take on a Re-Max franchise and was looking for new recruits for his new venture. With Re-Max the individuals worked on commission only, a percentage of which went to Re-Max and a percentage to the Franchisee (Terry), and after expenses what was left was yours. We were of course in England and working under English Law, and it has to be said it wasn't a great system then. I have no idea if it has changed since, but right up until the last minute the buyer or the seller could pull out and this left for a lot of frustration, anger and bitterness, on many occasions. So much so that after a while I felt it was completely beyond me to stay in such an unethical business with both buyers and sellers (not all them of course) playing cat and mouse, trying to get a few thousand up or down here or there, but at what cost?

I had completed all the training and was excited about my new career. I enjoyed meeting people, visiting their houses and making up a sales brochure for them. I also took on a shop window in the next town which was going to be my area. One man I was on a training course with called me the Bible Man (quite a complement really) he was fascinated to know how a Bible Man was going to get on as an Estate Agent, I was soon to discover what he meant.

Things started well, I had a few properties on my books and was looking forward to my sales commission. Unfortunately, it can take a while to sell houses and then take another while for the sale to go through before my commission would be paid. I was running up expenses quicker than the sales were coming through and I needed an income to pay the bills. I do not know how it happened, but I ended up with a job as a postman. At that time, a postman's job consisted of early starts, six days a week and meant you were nearly always finished by lunch time, leaving afternoons and evenings free for my estate agent job. As the newest postman in the office, I didn't have my own walk (round) and therefore started as cover for whatever rounds were available due to holidays or absences. I loved it, just sort your mail and then out in the fresh air on your bike and finish when you finish. At one point we had moved to Sutton-on-Sea and I could cycle along the seafront to the sorting office in Mablethorpe. There was one problem with it, snobbery. I sometimes used to deliver mail in Sutton-on-Sea and one or two of my clients and prospective clients did not like the idea that their 'estate agent' was a postman in his spare time. They were ok with their estate agent lying, cheating and changing the goalposts on deals time and again on their behalf, but not one who earned an honest living doing manual graft.

Things came to a head for me over two particular deals. One man had been happy to see a deal drag on to his benefit, he was building a second house and it wasn't finished, but once it was finished, he demanded the prospective buyer bought it straight away. He had kept this man hanging on in a chain until he was ready, the man was almost ready to complete when the seller said 'you've taken too long, give me another ten thousand and it's yours'. The buyer lived quite a bit away and it was probably just as well, his wife had been quite ill over the comings and goings of the deal, and he had had enough. The seller then said to me 'Ah well I'll just put it back on the market for another £10,000.' I said 'Not with me you won't', and walked out. This is how we treat one another to line our own pockets, it shouldn't be so and a society that allows such a system to exist should hang its head in shame.

A similar story happened with another client, I had worked hard to get him his asking price and when he got the offer he said 'I'm in no hurry to sell (he lived on a caravan on site) I think I'll put it on for more.' I said 'You can do that, but not with me.' I only got paid on completion of sale (we had a policy that the agent whose property it was showed the house, so a lot of running back and forward) and having houses on your books then off your books and back on again didn't look good. But the fact that these sellers wanted to back out and change deals almost on a whim just to see if they could squeeze a few thousand out of somebody; played havoc with people's mental health, and it was me the agent who had to do their dirty work. I decided enough was enough. I went into the office, gave the properties I had to any of the other agents who wanted them and walked out. I remember Dave one of the other agents say to me 'You can't just do that' I said, 'Watch me.' I left and never went back.

The next day I got up and went to work as a postman, an honest day's pay for an honest day's work. I could sleep easy at night with a clear conscience, you can't beat that. The promise of big money commission checks, well, you can keep them.

The sleep of a labouring man is sweet, Whether he eats little or much;
But the abundance of the rich will not permit him to sleep.
Ecclesiastes 5:12

23

A Three Storey House by the Sea

Delight yourself also in the LORD, and He shall give you the desires of your heart. Psalm 37:4

For a number of years, it had been our dream to 'retire' to a house by the sea. The way I had worked things out was our mortgage would be paid off by the time I was 52 and working in the Aerospace Industry there were always opportunities for redundancy or early retirement. We would sell our house and use the money to buy a house by the sea and my redundancy would pay for our simple lifestyle, eating, drinking and being merry.

And I will say to my soul, "Soul, you have many goods laid up for many years; take your ease; eat, drink, and be merry." Luke 12:19

Interestingly I am not the only person to have made plans for their future, but even more interesting is God's reaction to this man in the next verse.

But God said to him, 'Fool!' Luke 12:20

I have often heard it say if you want to give God a laugh, tell Him your plans. We are never as in control of our lives as we think we are and now here we were living in Lincolnshire in a small hamlet in the country, just outside a market town. The money from the sale of our house was about to run out (in timing with a Word we had from God in how long it would last). I was working as an estate agent and a postman and Jean was working in a care home to make ends meet (which they always did). Where was the dream now of a house by the sea? Where were the desires of our heart? Well now that we were living in God's Kingdom and our ways were committed to Him our dreams seemed irrelevant to us; but not to God.

I had just become the sales agent for a house in Sutton-on-Sea. It was a large three storey house with a large back garden and at the end of the garden there were steps which lead up to the sea wall and on to the beach. One day Jean and I were walking along the sea wall and we stopped to look at the house; we felt God was saying it was ours and that we were to use it to bless men and women of God and to be a place where people could come and draw aside from the busy-ness of the world and, in particular, ministry. But it was for sale and there was no way at this time we could afford to buy it. Jean said 'If God wants us to have it then it's ours'. We went to see the owner and after he had shown Jean and I around it (I obviously knew the house) we sat in one of the sun lounges (it had two) and talked to the owner and his wife. We explained to him the vision God had given us for the house and how we were to use it. Then we explained to them we had no money to buy it and asked would they consider renting it to us. They agreed, and right there and then they took down the 'for sale' sign and we made plans to rent it.

Delight yourself also in the LORD, And He shall give you the desires of your heart. Commit your way to the LORD, Trust also in Him, And He shall bring it to pass. Psalm 37:4-5

Now at the age of 42, and not retired, we had our house by the sea, God is good. We had some amazing times, in our 'house by the sea', including being host to a family of six from London who had felt called to the area but needed a base to stay as they searched for a house. There was also a young man who Jean met on the way back from the charity shop she helped run. It was pouring with rain and Jean met this young man soaked through without a jacket. She asked him in out of the rain; she tried to speak to him about Jesus but he was not managing to keep his eyes open so she said to him to go upstairs to bed and get some rest. When I came in from work and Jean said to me 'we have a visitor upstairs' I thought we had a mouse.

Jean explained to me about young Nathan and how he was just sleeping it off. He stayed with us for a while as we tried to help him but eventually he moved on and a few weeks later we saw his picture in the local paper. He was part of a drug dealing gang and had been sentenced to jail. We wrote to him a couple of times but lost touch. He was a gentle, polite young man and at no time did Jean ever fear him or be anxious about her safety. Some of that was God in Jean assuring her that He was with her, but some of it was that this young man was just a lost soul who could see the love of Christ in Jean and appreciated the unconditional acceptance he received in the name of Jesus.

Another story with a lighter side was when the owner's daughter was getting married, we were approached by them asking to be able to use the 'family home' for the girl to leave from. We were of course delighted to do this and left the house for the day and joined the family later at the wedding reception. After a couple of years, the owner decided he would like his house back, he had bought a house round the corner which he had renovated but now decided he would prefer to come 'home'. We agreed a swap and we moved into the house he renovated while he moved back to his three-storey house by the sea. We had had our season there, not by anything that we could do but by the grace of God. The house we moved into was a former minister's house and in fact when the owner had first moved in, he came across a lot of 'Holy Books' which he offered to us and which we gladly took. Now we were moving into this house formerly owned by a man of God and now being used for God's glory once again as we settled in, looking forward to what God had in store for us.

For I know the plans I have for you,' declares the LORD, 'plans to prosper you and not to harm you, plans to give you hope and a future.
Jeremiah 29:11 (NIVUK)

24

Life Begins When the Kids Leave Home and the Dog Dies, (Not)

To everything there is a season, A time for every purpose under heaven: Ecclesiastes 3:1

The world is full of little sayings, many of which come directly from the Bible. These are the useful ones (but that's another book) but a lot of them are just trying to cover up, by trivialising, something that has become a reality in your life that you would prefer not to be reality, and they are of no use at all. The name of this chapter comes from empty nesters trying to convince themselves that life is just about to get really good, and that there is still meaning to their days ahead. It is often seen on the back of caravans or camper vans, the ultimate sign of 'freedom'. Well, it doesn't say a lot to your kids, other than you're glad to see the back of them, and that your whole life has been on hold waiting for them to get out of the way. Not a nice message and (in most cases) completely untrue. So why say it? Probably fear, fear of not being needed, fear that our best days may actually be behind us and not ahead, fear that somehow the meaning behind our lives for the past twenty or so years has just gone and that we need some new meaning to our lives, and do we have one?

The above happened to us at completely the wrong and unexpected time, as life often does. We were living in Sutton-on-Sea and our daughter Kerry had a boyfriend from school who lived in another town. In Lincolnshire that generally means awkward travelling arrangements, especially for teenagers. Kerry seemed to be more at her boyfriend's than he was at ours and we kept insisting she had to come home. One night she insisted that she was staying at her boyfriend's and during a heated phone call I said something that came out all wrong and gave her an open door to react all wrong and rebellious, making the situation worse instead of better. I said, 'If you don't come home tonight, don't bother coming home at all'. Why do fathers say such stupid things to hot headed teenagers? She did not come home, it was a disastrous outcome and one which I wish had never happened, but it did.

During the time my daughter was away, our dog became more and more ill until the point where the vet recommended we have her put down. We had had her for nearly fourteen years. We told Kerry, who came home to see her dog and then we had our dog put down. The 'kid had left home and the dog had died', now what? It was devastating, the dog wasn't coming back but we were determined our daughter was, we loved her and wanted the best for her and this situation wasn't the best. After talking to her, we asked if we moved to Spilsby would she come home? This was the town where her then boyfriend lived, and they would be able to visit each other regularly. She wanted to see the house we were moving to, which by the grace of God was a brand new fully furnished house which she 'approved of'. I got a transfer of work (postman) to Spilsby, Jean and I moved there and Kerry returned back home. The things we do for the love of our children.

The next time Kerry moved out was to go to Aston University in Birmingham. This time we were prepared for it, but it was still hard. It may be a new season when your children move out but it is not when 'life begins', life is a continuous journey and has many seasons to be enjoyed. Enjoy each season for what it is, and do not spoil the previous season by trivialising it or making out that the next season is what you are waiting for. Life is what happens when you're waiting for the next season, don't miss the now.

Kerry was to 'leave' us again to get married to Andrew and we now have two amazing grandsons. Without letting go of the past seasons, we can miss much of the present season. Even when we make a huge mistake, God can still work it out that we can enjoy the next season.

And we know that all things work together for good to those who love God, to those who are the called according to His purpose.
Romans 8:28

Girls School to University

Train up a child in the way he should go, and when she is old she will not depart from it. Proverbs 22:6

Training up a child in the way they should go involves training them up in the house by the parents but also requires us to be sending them to the right school. As we moved a lot during Kerry's school years the choice of school was not always in our hands but we are firm believers in the local school so as we moved around Kerry was put into the local school.

When we left France to come back to England to go to Bible college this was going to be in God's hands and as has been so often the case in our walk with God, they proved to be the best hands. Kerry's first school move was at the age of seven when we moved from Tarbolton to Ayr and she left the local village school to go to Holmston Primary, which was next door to our house. Then at the age of nine came her big move.

We moved to France and, having taken advice, we enrolled her in the local village school in Pibrac where we lived. She was the only English-speaking pupil there and she spoke no French, it was a real baptism of fire for her, but she excelled. After being there for a few weeks, there was a school trip going to Biarritz for a few days which she went to, rather shell shocked but she went along with it. I think she coped better with it than Jean who wanted me to drive her to Biarritz just to see how Kerry was doing. When Kerry came home, we asked her how she had got on, she said 'I learned to say 'it wasn't me' in French'. She went on to become fluent in French to this day and to have many good French friends, one of whom came to her wedding in Scotland.

From there Kerry went to the Lycee Victor Hugo in Colomiers, a French secondary school. Then we got saved and we were heading back to England, Horsham in West Sussex to be precise. There we put Kerry in the Millais which turns out to be the best secondary school in the area, praise God. It also turned out to be an all-girls school, another challenge for Kerry as she had never experienced an all-girls school, but she rose to the challenge. After two years there we were on the move again, this time to Lincolnshire, where Kerry went to a Grammar school which required an entrance exam which she passed, and from there she left to go to Aston University having risen once again to the challenge of a new school, new friends and new life. Kerry was always very resilient, and due to her nature always readily accepted and welcomed in all these different surroundings, for which we thank God.

She has now settled in Cheshire with her husband Andrew and two sons, Rufus and Axel, and we thank God for them all every day, but especially for Kerry who has come through it all as our bright and shining star.

Behold, children are a heritage from the Lord, The fruit of the womb is a reward. Psalm 127:3

Kerry has been and still is a wonderful reward from God.

1996 – I'm Never Going Back to Scotland. 2006 – Going Back to Scotland

(Do Not Boast About Tomorrow)
Come now, you who say, "Today or tomorrow we will go to such and such a city, spend a year there, buy and sell, and make a profit";
James 4:13

There are lots of reasons we decide to leave places and not to return, sometimes we are chasing a dream, or sometimes bad experiences, painful memories, or we don't like the weather, we don't like the people, we can't see a future there, or we think our children would be better off elsewhere, more opportunities for them and for us as a family, and on and on. But there is also the running away reason, not running away from anything in particular, (although we can usually come up with something in one of the above categories to justify it), but just running away from life. But guess what, yes that's right, life has a habit of following you. I had a picture of Scotland that said it was drab, dreary and grey. Now, don't get me wrong, some days when you look out your window it can look very much like that. But now I had a chance to move to France and sunshine and brightness and a dry climate and I made an inward vow that I would never go back to Scotland to live, I was finished with it once and for all. But God was about to show me that weather does not make the man.

We had been living in France nearly two years and things on the surface were good, but underneath was still just as rotten as when I left Scotland. It was at this point that God showed me that it wasn't Scotland that was drab, dreary and grey but my heart, ouch! Now came the challenge, was I going to deal with it? Was I going to let Jesus into my heart? Was I going to let the 'Son' shine in my heart? I always say that at this point I nearly never became a Christian. I had the opportunity to change but it would involve looking inside and seeing what I was really like, was I prepared to do this? Eventually yes, why eventually? Well sometimes we can get quite comfortable with our misery, it can be hard work to change but I was to find out that not only did God want me to change but that He did not expect me to do it on my own, He would give me His Holy Spirit who would teach and enable me to deal with things. He would give me a Spirit filled couple to help get things out and most of all He would give me a Godly woman who would stand by me and encourage me and love me while I changed. That woman would be the 'wife of my youth' who had been through so much junk with me but with her faith in Jesus Christ, empowered by the Holy Spirit, and by God's grace she would stand by me.

Yet you say, "For what reason?" Because the Lord has been witness Between you and the wife of your youth, With whom you have dealt treacherously; Yet she is your companion And your wife by covenant. But did He not make them one, Having a remnant of the Spirit? And why one? He seeks godly offspring. Therefore, take heed to your spirit, and let none deal treacherously with the wife of his youth.
Malachi 2:14-15

In 2006, ten years after we had left Scotland, with me saying I would never return to that drab, dreary, grey place, God called us to go back. But with my new heart and not the drab, dreary, grey one I had left with, Scotland became my home again. God would work in my heart to such an extent that eight years later when He would ask us to leave Scotland again, this time to live in England, I would find it hard to leave but would do so with fond memories of our time there.

6 Months in Scotland (2006 – 2014)

A man's heart plans his way, But the LORD directs his steps.
Proverbs 16:9

For the more observant of you I won't have to point out that 2006 – 2014 is more than 6 months; man makes his plans but God directs his steps. When back in Scotland visiting family for Christmas 2005, we realised that Jean's family were really struggling coping with her father's decreasing mobility after his stroke in 2001. We decided we needed to go back to Scotland and help out, the deal was we would go back for six months and help out. Who the deal was with I have no idea, but we ended up back there for just over six years.

We were living in Spilsby, Lincolnshire and Kerry was now at Aston University in Birmingham. We left our jobs, packed everything we had into our Volvo and headed back to Scotland. Not only were we going back to the village where we both grew up, but we were going to be living in the house which Jean had been brought up in and, on top of that, we were going to be living in the room in which Jean had been born. Talk about going back to your roots. We had no furniture; God had prepared us six months earlier when we moved into a fully furnished rental house. We gave away all our furniture including white goods. I had thought about selling some of it on eBay, but Jean felt we should give it away and I agreed. We contacted a charity in Mablethorpe called Furnichurch. They take in donated items and give them away to families in need. So, we headed back to Scotland with all our worldly goods. Unlike when we left France to come back to England it did not take a large Pickford's truck, it only took our old trusty Volvo estate, bought off eBay.

We spent the next eighteen months looking after Jean's dad before he passed away, it was hard at times, but it was a privilege. I became his personal carer doing things for my father-in-law that neither he nor I would have ever thought would happen. He was a gracious and patient invalid which made it easier for those looking after him, but it could not have been easy for him. He was an ex-miner and had lived and worked in a 'man's world' and now he had to submit to others attending to his personal needs. Our main focus was that he wouldn't have to go into a care home and could live the rest of his life at home, this we managed. But more challenges were to come.

Jean's mum was diagnosed with vascular dementia and despite living with her for a further three years (almost five years in total), we finally had to give in and allow her to be taken in to care in a local nursing home. This was on the instructions of Social Services who by this time had legal guardianship over Nan's care. We had been advised to do this as we would not make the decision in a timely fashion and would base our good intentions on emotions and not on Nan's care. My wife struggled with this decision at the time and has gone back to it from time to time, but has finally put it in God's hands. Nan lived in the home for seven years; by the end she was totally bed ridden, didn't recognise anyone and could make no understandable communication. But she was at peace and for that we can only be grateful to God, whom she knew as her loving saviour. Nan went into the home at the end of 2010 and we continued to live in the family home. In 2011, after I finished my degree at the University of Glasgow, we went on a pilgrimage, walking the Camino de Santiago. On our return, we believed it was right now to leave the family home; Nan was obviously never going to be well enough to come home. We left the house and made plans to leave Scotland and return to England. That was at the end of 2011, in March 2014 we finally moved back to England after spending over two years in Girvan: for those of you unfamiliar with Girvan, it is in Scotland, man makes his plans but God directs his steps.

Why Are You Driving Past My Church?

(The Joy of Going to the House of the Lord. A Song of Ascents. Of
David).
*I was glad when they said to me, "Let us go into the house of
the Lord."* Psalm 122:1

When we headed back to Scotland, we moved back to our old village
of Tarbolton, which had two churches: a Brethren church, 'the Gospel
Hall', and the Parish Church, which was Church of Scotland. The Parish
Church was the one which we had both been brought up in, our fathers
were elders in it, our parents had been married in it, we had been
'christened' in it and married in it and we had our daughter 'christened'
in it. But in 1994 we had left the village with no ties whatsoever with
the church. Now in 2006, we had no intention of going back to it. We
were 'born again', Spirit-filled Christians and we were heading off to
Prestwick where there was an AOG church with like-minded Christians.
To do this we had to drive past the Parish Church every Sunday until
one day we felt God was saying to us 'Why are you driving past my
church?' We felt convicted and started going to the local Parish Church
which meant we could take Jean's dad to it. Since his stroke, he had
been unable to attend the church, but with us to help we were able to
take him in his wheelchair. Whilst we were there, we ran an Alpha
Course and started a drop in café for the youth who nicknamed it the
'Jesus Café'.

Also during our time there I ended up at the University of Glasgow
studying Theology and Religious Studies. Alex, the minister there, came
to us one evening and said he thought I had a call on my life and had I
considered the ministry? I ended up exploring ministry within the
Church of Scotland, but it wasn't to be. After going through the

selection process, I was turned down. The minister in Troon who I had been under for six months asked me if I would apply again but I said 'no I thought the decision was right'. The Church of Scotland had moved so far away from the things I believed that I felt it was time to leave it. Jean's dad had passed on by this time and that season was now over. On our last Sunday at the church, I felt God give me a word for not just that church but for the Church of Scotland as a whole. They had been talking over the 'homosexual issue' at the General Assembly once again, and once again they put it off until the next year's General Assembly for further talks without making any decision. I stood up one Sunday in my home church and boldly proclaimed.

So then, because you are lukewarm, and neither a] cold nor hot, I will vomit you out of My mouth. Revelation 3:16

This was something out of character for me, and definitely not something done in the local Church of Scotland; it was the last time we went to that church and the last time we had anything to do with the Church of Scotland.

What a Friend We Have in Jesus

Greater love has no one than this, than to lay down one's life for his friends. You are My friends if you do whatever I command you. No longer do I call you servants, for a servant does not know what his master is doing; but I have called you friends, for all things that I heard from My Father I have made known to you. John 15:13-15

I spent all of my adult life slowly getting more and more addicted to drink, to the point where I did not function without a drink in my hand. I had become relatively successful; good job, nice house with a swimming pool, 4x4, the trappings of success were there but so was the trap of alcohol. Alcohol had been with me my whole journey but had not brought any satisfaction with it, only misery, until at the age of 40 having become a Christian I slowly was able to let go. Through the power of the Holy Spirit I was released from my need for alcohol and the false expectation that somehow drink was the answer.

During our time as Christians God has placed many people in our path who quickly became close friends. One friend we made as Christians had a very different story as far as his relationship with alcohol was concerned. He had worked hard and also had the trappings of success; he had his own caravan at a site where he could take the family to at the weekends but suddenly at the age of 40 he found himself using alcohol to 'help him relax'. He had never been a drinker until then and it quickly became an obsession with him. By the time we met him in 2006 he had become a full-blown alcoholic. He had had an encounter with Jesus and had been in and out of recovery homes, but always relapsed. He was from the same village as Jean and I and we knew him and his family, not well, but in a 'villagey' sort of way, where everyone is known by everyone else to some degree. We also knew his wife who was from the same village as well. We met him at Newlife Church in Prestwick and were blown away by his testimony and what God had done in his life. His wife was a 'good person' and didn't need God whereas her husband obviously did (her words). Then one day she accompanied him to church and spent the whole service crying, she too saw her need for a saviour who loved her and wanted to change her life. Unknown to Jean, his wife had been praying for us for years while we were still living in France, often asking Jean's dad how we were doing, thank God for her faithful prayers.

The effective, fervent prayer of a righteous man (or woman) avails much. James 5:16b

We would go to their house for some fellowship with others and he would play the guitar and lead worship. One of his favourite songs, which also became one of mine, is the song 'What a friend we have in Jesus.' We had some good times, then we would get the phone call to say 'he was back on the drink'. When he drank, he drank hard, no dabbling, just straight back on and he got into some terrible states.

Early one morning we went round to see him after a particularly hard session; he was lying on the couch recovering. Jean gave him a word from the Lord, 'God will not be mocked.' His reply, 'That was what Pastor Alwyn said.' He had received the same word just days earlier. He was professing Christ, going to church, worshipping and praising God and crawling about the streets (literally) asking for money for more drink. He even asked me one morning to get him a quarter bottle of whisky just to straighten him out. His witness in our small community was that God was not able. Within a few weeks, at the age of 52, he was found dead. He went out for a walk in the country, sat down on a bench and died. He had a good Christian funeral, we believe he is in heaven today praising God, but how he could not beat that demon drink. Only he and God know, something inside him ate away at him and eventually killed him. That is why it is so important for us to get everything out in the open and let God deal with it, leaving no stone unturned, receiving God's full forgiveness and believing God's promise of a new life. We have to believe and live out what is declared to us in God's word.

Therefore, if anyone is in Christ, he is a new creation; old things have passed away; behold, all things have become new. 2 Corinthians 5:17

Whatever we hold onto whatever 'old things' we do not let pass away, they have the potential to come back and get us. A song he liked, and which was played at his funeral, was 'Lord I hope this day is good'. It contains the lyrics:

Lord, I hope this day is good
I'm feelin' empty and misunderstood
I should be thankful Lord, I know I should
But Lord, I hope this day is good
Lord, have you forgotten me?
I've been prayin' to you faithfully
I'm not sayin' I'm a righteous man
But Lord, I hope you understand.

It's a nice enough song but contains no faith, and even the line 'I hope this day is good' seems to be one of hopeless hope rather than faith-filled hope. But the line that strikes me is not the catchy chorus above but the one that says, 'I'm not sayin' I'm a righteous man'. We as Christians should not be declaring this over our lives, we should actually be declaring that we are righteous, not in our own good, but in Christ Jesus. We should be declaring the word of God over our lives which declares that we are the righteousness of God in Christ Jesus:

For He made Him who knew no sin to be sin for us, that we might become the righteousness of God in Him.(Jesus). 2 Corinthians 5:21

It is by grace through faith in Jesus Christ that we can declare we are righteous. It is a gift from God, but we have to receive that gift and believe it by faith.

For by grace you have been saved through faith, and that not of yourselves; it is the gift of God, not of works, lest anyone should boast.
Ephesians 2:8-9

Despite everything, his wife's faith remained firm and to this day she is a committed Christian. Praise God.

Kilcreggan – The Way Christian Ministries

And I also say to you that you are Peter, and on this rock I will build
My church, and the gates of Hades shall not prevail against it.
Matthew 16:18

The telling of our friend's death in the previous chapter reminds me of where we were when we got the news. We were volunteering at a ministry in Kilcreggan; when Jean received the phone call from our friend's wife it was devastating, but good to be among more Christian friends. Peter and Nancy Stanway, along with their son Israel and other volunteers, ran The Way Christian Ministries from, at that time, Kilcreggan House. Peter has his own fascinating testimony which he tells in his book, *Wee Boys From Glasgow Don't Cry* (which is available on Amazon.). The name of the ministry is one of the best I know and to top it all, the name of the house and village he ran it from, Kilcreggan, means 'church on the little rock.' And then of course his name is Peter. Unfortunately, we have lost touch with Peter, we know he moved from Kilcreggan to Largs and was heavily involved in a work in Spain where he lived when he first became a Christian. How we came to know Peter and Nancy and end up giving some time to volunteer was just one of those 'God Things'. We were at Faith Camp in Peterborough when we met this larger-than-life Christian from Scotland. The accents are always enough for our ears to prick up and get talking to someone from 'home'. We clicked immediately, as most people do with Peter, but it would be some time later when we were back in Scotland that we would visit them in Kilcreggan.

Peter was from Glasgow and Nancy was from Ayrshire, where we came from, and one day after having moved back to Scotland they dropped in on us and spent some time with us, praying for Jean's dad who had a stroke and her mum who later was diagnosed with Dementia, a condition which she already had the early signs of. They looked after Nancy's dad who had dementia and understood the difficulties of living and caring for parents. We then went to visit them to see the work they were doing. They had a couple of interns helping out throughout the week but their busiest time was at the weekend when they had various churches and Christian groups coming for retreats and Alpha weekends. After praying about it and looking at how it fitted in with helping Jean's mum and dad, we ended up volunteering to help at weekends. We would travel up on Fridays, help finish preparations for the coming guests and help with cleaning, cooking and serving over the weekend, helping strip the beds and do the laundry before returning home on the Sunday evening.

Travelling was fun, we had to get a lift to the nearest station (7 miles) and then took two trains and a ferry to get there. It was a blessed time and one we were grateful for. It gave us a break from caring for Jeans parents before the time came when we had to give it up to be there for them more and more. One travel adventure I remember was a particularly rocky ferry journey. It was a fairly short journey across the Clyde from Gourock to Kilcreggan but this day it was looking pretty rough. Instead of heading straight across, we zigzagged our way across as the ship tossed up and down. We normally rode on the top of the ship with our case as it was too narrow and steep a staircase to get down with a case but this time we had been advised we needed to go 'down below' for this crossing. As our case was too big to get down the stairs, the seaman strapped it to the railing. We kept looking out the window as we made our way across the Clyde expecting our suitcase to go flying past us at any minute, it did not, and we arrived there safely. It was one of the last trips for that ferry as it was soon to be replaced by a more modern type. Progress isn't always for the best; the old ferry had character.

We were to meet many characters at Kilcreggan House including a 'Christian Clown', a submariner (from the nearby submarine base) and many genuine Christians who were looking for that something more in their Christian walk. I believe they would have found it at 'The Way'.

And you will seek Me and find Me, when you search for Me with all your heart. Jeremiah 29:13

Because Jean Asked Me To

I will set nothing wicked before my eyes; Psalm 101:3

There are some things in life you just never get around to, and not for any reason other than you just plain don't want to. Writing this chapter is one of those and the only reason I am writing it is because 'Jean asked me to.' This book is set to record the good, the bad and the ugly of our journey and this chapter is the downright ugly. Not just because of what happened, which was bad enough, but the fact that I was now a professing Christian and it happened. Being a Christian may help in knowing what is right and wrong but when it all comes down to it, you still have the choice of doing what is right or wrong. When the pressure is on, when something bad is happening, when everything is just too much, are you going to get down on your knees and trust God or are you going to buckle completely and revert to type? Even though your type no longer is part of who you are or who you should be, now that you are a new creation in Christ Jesus.

So how does it happen, how does the devil get in? Well to be honest, we open a door and the devil rushes in, he doesn't hesitate, he doesn't give you time to take a breath, he just starts up the roller coaster and before you know it, you're on the road to hell. If that sounds a bit too dramatic then ask someone you know who fell, where it started and how many wrong choices it took them to get there, and you'll find out it took them fewer wrong choices than they ever thought as they got sucked in quicker than they ever thought and stayed longer than they ever thought.

But this is a personal book so what happened to me? How did I get so lost so quickly? The main answer to that has to be not sticking to my faith as much as I should, and relying more on my wife's faith than my own. This meant when push came to shove, my roots weren't deep enough, my foundation was not on the rock of Jesus Christ, it was on driftwood. When I was at school, one of the teachers said to me "you're a drifter boy and the first storm you hit you will sink you." I was now in a storm and I was gathering as much driftwood together as I could, because I was not going to sink, I was going to drift on. The storms were coming thick and fast; I had just spent eighteen months caring for my father-in-law, doing things for him that you never dream that you will do for your father-in-law. Now I was looking at going forward for ministry with the Church of Scotland and preparing to speak in my home church which I grew up in and where both Jean and my parents attended along with relatives, friends and neighbours, most of whom were aware of my background in drinking and partying. In the midst of all this, Jean spent three weeks in hospital with an unknown, unidentifiable skin disease which had the possibility of being life threating and at the very least debilitating.

Somewhere along the line I lost the plot. I remember one night on the way home from the hospital buying two small bottles of wine, the 330ml size. It had been two years since I had had a drink and whereas before this wouldn't even have whet my appetite, alone in a room with a computer it was deadly. I was just trying to shut everything off, a little numbing of the pain, where could it possibly lead to? All the way to hell and back actually. I can't to this day put a timeline on anything or how quickly it all became a mess, but that day when Jean went on the computer and saw the history it was like my whole world collapsed.

That wasn't the worst of it, Jean's whole world collapsed, again, and it was all down to me, again. No hard-core porn but a list that got steadily more and more degrading until the final degradation, names from my past that we knew. What was I trying to find out? What was I looking for? Some sort of twisted respite from my present situation? Why was I not looking to Jesus? Was I looking to make contact? No. I had no interest at all in that. I was piling up driftwood that I was looking to get me through a storm, but all the while I was really piling up firewood that the devil was going to use to roast me alive.

Men think fantasy is an escape but it's not, it's a door. A door that the devil will rush in, sit down and set up camp. The devil didn't make me do it, drink didn't make me do it, the situations I was in or had been in or was going to be in, didn't make me do it. I chose to do it, and the only thing I got out of it was guilt and pain, and the greatest pain, destroying the trust of my wife Jean, again. Anyone who tells you looking is harmless is a liar; looking shuts down your true feelings in a situation, it shuts down the Holy Spirit working in your life, it shuts down intimacy with the love of your life and can ultimately lead to a complete collapse of that relationship. I am blessed to have a wife who does not understand but chooses to forgive and show me the grace and mercy that God has shown her. No other relationship can inspire us to be like that, other than a real relationship with Jesus Christ. If we put our relationship with Jesus Christ first, then everything else comes into place. But only if we keep choosing to put Him first and choosing to resist temptations will we be overcomers.

'Therefore submit to God. Resist the devil and he will flee from you.'
James 4:7

32

You Will Not Smell of Smoke

the hair of their head was not singed nor were their garments affected, and the smell of fire was not on them. Daniel 3:27

In the previous chapter I mentioned that Jean spent three weeks in hospital with a skin disease. This came completely out of the blue, Jean started feeling itchy, this turned into feeling itchy all over to the point where it was driving her crazy. The doctors couldn't pinpoint anything, and after various blood tests and a biopsy with it just getting worse, she ended up in hospital. By this time, Jean's skin looked like she had been scalded. It was on her hands and arms and legs and even on her eyelids. In the hospital she had to be wrapped from head to foot in bandages every day to stop the itch; the doctors were baffled, and they sent her records to London to see what they could come up with. Almost every day a new group of doctors and student doctors and nurses would come to see the strange phenomenon which was Jean's illness. They even took pictures of her, which we still have a copy of.

Jean's faith was strong throughout, so much so that the hospital chaplain used to visit her for some encouragement. She would tell doctors and nurses and anyone who would listen that God was going to heal her and was a constant source of encouragement for those around her; one woman who was being discharged was now heading back home to go to church where she had never been for years. Jean was sent for scans and MRIs as they were checking for underlying cancer as the cause, they found nothing. Jean was unphased by it all, even when on the way for a scan to check for cancer it was cancelled at the last minute and put off until the next day.

Jean got a word from the Lord 'you will not even smell of smoke'. Jean took this to mean that when all this was over there would be no trace of any skin disease. With the state her body was in, this definitely looked most unlikely. Her skin looked scalded, then the steroids kicked in and her legs were swollen. To return to complete normality after this was going to take a miracle.

Jean was eventually released and given tablets for her condition, she had to attend a specialist as an outpatient at a nearby hospital. One day a woman we know appeared at Jean's mum's house where we staying and said she had been on the bus and the Lord laid it on her heart to come and pray with Jean. She felt to lay hands on her and take Communion and believe for her complete healing, all of which they did. Jean's skin cleared and she told her doctor that Jesus had healed her, and that she was coming of the tablets. The specialist advised her that she would have to take the tablets for the rest of her life and that if she didn't it would flare up. Jean said she was healed and that she would take full responsibility for the outcome of not taking the tablets. The doctor was furious and left the room, the nurse couldn't believe that Jean had said that to the doctor. When he returned, he gave Jean a 24-hour emergency telephone number and said you will need this it will return when you stop taking these tablets and you will have to come back in.

Jean never needed the emergency number but had to continue attending the clinic to keep an eye on her condition. On her last visit, as the doctor was signing her off, he said 'Well Jean, you got your miracle'. There was no sign or mark left by the disease on her body, she was completely healed 'and did not even smell of smoke'. We serve a miracle working God and all praise and glory go to Him and His son Jesus.

who Himself bore our sins in His own body on the tree, that we, having died to sins, might live for righteousness—by whose stripes you were healed. 1 Peter 2:24

A (Scottish) Wedding from Scratch (In Just Two Months)

Therefore a man shall leave his father and mother and be joined to his wife, and they shall become one flesh. Genesis 2:24

As our daughter Kerry was coming near to the end of her time at university she came home one Christmas break with her boyfriend Andrew, she told us that they had decided that after university they were going to rent a place and live together. As committed Christians we were horrified, as you can imagine, or perhaps you can't. After all everybody is doing it?

Our belief, which we get from the Bible, is that God's best plan for us if we are going to be living with someone in a love relationship is marriage. Kerry was adamant. When they came back up at Easter, I spoke to them again and explained we only wanted the best for them and moving in wasn't the best for them; God wanted so much more than they could ever imagine. In June they phoned with the news they were engaged, Praise God! But the battle was not over, they were still intending to move in and have their wedding the following year in August. I explained to Kerry, that's not a wedding, that's a day out. She said that they couldn't afford a wedding that quick, that was when I heard myself say 'We will pay everything.' That was definitely a faith statement, we didn't have the money either, but God. It was left at that. Then on the 1st of July we got a phone call, if it could be done they wanted to do it this August.

God was going to have to do a few miracles here, Kerry had a list of what she wanted for her wedding and it was going to take some doing. We prayed hard and started on her list.

She wanted her wedding reception in the Brig O' Doon, a very popular hotel for weddings and usually booked a year in advance, sometimes two if you wanted it in such a popular month. They had nothing at the weekend but had Monday 31st August available, an English bank holiday, it suited well with Kerry as Andrew was English and his relatives would be able to make it. Tick. She wanted to use the Auld Kirk in Alloway instead of our own Parish Church in Tarbolton, it was still a Church of Scotland church, and we got it. Tick. She said we could not get a cake made in time. We got a baker in Troon to make one. Tick. She wanted four bridesmaids, we agreed. Tick. Andrew wanted two best men, no problem. Tick. A dress, how could she get one of those on time? She came home and the first dress she saw she loved, it was just like the one she had picked out in a wedding magazine, (and on sale). Tick.

She eventually agreed it was possible and we went for it. Kerry made her own favours and table decorations based on the theme of Scottish Tartans. We arranged a Scottish Ceilidh band and the whole day was a great success. Jean and I danced the night away at the reception having only to rely on water and the grace of God instead of alcohol. Andrew and his two best men were dressed in full highland dress; whilst getting ready one of them said 'it seems strange to be putting a dagger down my sock to go to a wedding'.

It was such a privilege to take my daughter down the aisle and give her to the man she loved to start her new life. They are just about to celebrate their 10th wedding anniversary by going to Paris, leaving Nana and Papa to look after the two grandsons, that's after spending a short break with us as a whole family in a caravan in Scotland.

Oh, did I mention it rained on their wedding day? (well it was a Scottish wedding) but that was no problem, they loved it, Andrew suffers from hay fever, he had no problem with it that day and one of their, and our, favourite photographs is them walking from the church to the reception under an umbrella.

It had taken just two months to arrange a complete wedding and with nothing left off our daughters list, God is good!!!!

A Biker for Jesus?

He who finds a wife finds a good thing, And obtains favour from the Lord. Proverbs 18:22

There are certain things in life that, left to our own devices, we just never get around to. There are always other priorities, other places for our money to go, other excuses, like I'm too old. And of course there is pride as well, what will people think of me? will they think I'm just going through a midlife crisis? Will I look stupid?

The Christmas after my 50th birthday my wife cut through all that and presented me with my CBT, no not Cognitive behavioural therapy (CBT) although she probably would have been justified in it, but COMPULSORY BASIC TRAINING: (CBT), for a motorcycle. Apart from wearing a few leather biker jackets in my day I had never got round to doing anything about actual motorcycle riding. When I was 17, I jumped in a car and had been there ever since. One of my friends bough a Honda 250 Superdream, jumped on it and rode of on a provisional licence, those were the days. Now I had to do a training course just to get on a 125cc. Having had two attempts to get through my CBT, I couldn't help but think about all those seventeen-year-olds jumping on a 250cc with a top speed of 85mph with no required training. My 125cc with a top speed of 65mph (downhill with a tail wind) was quite enough for me as a learner.

After I passed my CBT I bought a Chinese import 125cc, it was a great bike and a real looker. I didn't feel at all embarrassed about being the old man on a 125cc, it was great fun. I kept it for a year, using it for work and getting to my volunteer job as a presenter with Ayr Hospital Radio. I never took it any further and regrettably that is my entire experience as a 'biker', but I am for ever grateful to Jean my wife for pushing me to try it and it is an experience I will never forget. Throughout my life Jean has always come up with surprises like that, encouraging me to go for what I myself would not go for and would have left on the back burner until the flame went out. Driving Route 66 was a big one and something else that without Jean would have passed me by. It is one of Jean's gifts that I so love about her.

Who can find a virtuous wife? For her worth is far above rubies.
Proverbs 31:10

A DJ for Jesus

The voice of one crying in the wilderness: "Prepare the way of the Lord; Make straight in the desert A highway for our God. Isaiah 40:3

I am certainly not John the Baptist, but I did feel like a voice crying in the wilderness at times during my stint as a presenter at Ayr Hospital Radio. This was another case of me thinking out loud and Jean coming up behind me and encouraging me to step out in faith and see what happened. I had seen the advertisement for AHR while visiting the hospital and that they had slots available for new presenters but, well, maybe not. Then Jean, and before I knew it, I was in for an interview with Mike the CEO. The position was mine: Wednesdays 7 – 9pm, you can't talk about politics, religion or Rangers and Celtic. OH!

In my teenage years I had helped run a small mobile disco, we did the Scout Hall and a few outside events. But to be honest I was no DJ, I played some records and eyed up the girls. I did not speak through the microphone other than to make announcements, 'If you're going for the last bus, you've missed it', and other lame jokes. I had no 'patter'. Now I was going to be on air and 'patter' was to be part of my brief. But now they had taken most of my patter options away, 'no religion'. I went along for a few training sessions; the music was played mostly from CDs but was moving towards computers and they by this time had an extensive playlist on a PC. But I noticed that they had a large selection of now mostly redundant vinyl LP's; I was in heaven.

The first time I was on my own I started digging through the LP's, I like country music and there was a vast selection of old country and western albums. Now if you don't know much about the old country artists then I'll let you into a secret, most of them have 'religious' content on their albums. I settled down to selecting some of these songs. Now my audience profile was completely unknown, but you've got to think, hospital patients – a lot of them are going to be older, a lot of them are going to need some reassurance, some comfort and some peace. They needed Jesus. I wasn't supposed to talk about religion, but hey, Jesus isn't into religion either and I was only introducing their (AHR) records. It wasn't as if I was slyly introducing my own music with my own agenda. I was simply introducing songs, like: 'Lord I hope this day is good', 'One Day At a Time Sweet Jesus', 'What a Friend we have in Jesus', 'Old Rugged Cross', 'I am a Seeker', 'Poems Prayers and Promises', 'I Believe', and 'Blow up Your TV' (which includes the line 'Try and find Jesus on your own') to name but a few.

Whilst playing and introducing these you can't help but mention your faith and what God and Jesus means to you. Whether anybody got any comfort from it or whether anybody even heard any of it only God knows, but we are all called to be 'a voice crying out in the wilderness' and I was just doing my part.

A Degree, Who Me?

And further, my son, be admonished by these. Of making many books there is no end, and much study is wearisome to the flesh.
Ecclesiastes 12:12

In 2009 I started the process of exploring a calling to ministry within the Church of Scotland. This required me to have a theological degree from one of four acceptable universities in Scotland. While I was not required to start this prior to my acceptance by the Church of Scotland, because of my age and possible time limits involved in completing any training, I decided to enrol for a Bachelor of Divinity at the University of Glasgow and start that year at the same time as I was going through the selection process for ministry. As it happened, I did not pass the selection process and was subsequently turned down by the Church of Scotland. But, having started my degree I decided to carry on.

When I applied to the University of Glasgow, I was told that as I had insufficient qualifications (and what I had was ancient history, having left school in 1977, thirty-two years ago) I would have to attend summer school at the university. I had to pick four subjects, one of which, Study Skills, was compulsory, and I had to obtain a minimum of four B's. From a rather limited list I chose English Literature, German, Psychology and Study Skills. As I mentioned it was thirty-two years since I left school with some pretty poor results. I had passed my 'O' levels fairly easily but when it came to my Highers I failed miserably and even at a second attempt struggled to get pass marks. However, that was more down to lack of effort on my part than lack of brains. I just expected everything to come to me and if it required work then, too bad, I would just have to do without.

A 'floating' policy I would live with for the next 20 years before God, through my wife Jean, rocked my boat and made me realise that anything in life that is worth having (especially relationships) you are going to have to put some effort in and work at it. I obtained two A's and two B's and I was accepted for enrolment in the Theology and Religious Studies Course at the University of Glasgow.

The only thing I remember about the summer school was our first class on study skills. We were sitting in a circle and the lecturer was asking each person their name and where they came from. The boy next to me said he was from Dunfermline, the lecturer then just into the air asked what's the best thing to come out of Dunfermline, to which I piped up 'Dan McCafferty', 'Who's he?' he said, 'The lead singer with Nazareth' I replied. To which the boy from Dunfermline said, 'Oh, my best friend's grandfather is the lead guitarist'. Well, that dated me right away; if there was any doubt before that I was a 'really mature' student, there was no doubt now. It wasn't his friend's father, but it was his friend's grandfather who was in the band.

I went on to complete my degree finding it extremely interesting, I particularly took to studying in the library with a vast array of Christian books at my disposal. With it being a 'social science', I had a lot of leeway in my choice of some of my essays but also had some challenges on writing to more specific criteria. All in all it was a great three years and an experience I thoroughly enjoyed. In your first year you have to choose one subject from outside your area of study, I chose Celtic Civilisation. I was surprised how much of what we take as authentically 'Celtic' is very much just bits and pieces loosely joined together. The other thing about choosing a subject outside your area of study meant that a lot of first year students enrolled in one of our classes, 'World Religions', nearly two hundred students attended to hear about Islam, Judaism and Christianity. The most disappointing thing to me was while Islam and Judaism were spoken of in terms of a religion, Christianity was spoken of in terms of splits and divisions amongst it, particularly the Reformation. It was more a history of the church than the story of the one true God and His son Jesus Christ, such a huge opportunity to preach the Gospel and tell the Good News to hungry, eager to learn youngsters wasted.

I graduated in June 2011 at the age of 51, having never been to a University when I was younger, with an MA in Theology and Religious Studies, with distinction.

The motto of the University of Glasgow is 'Via, Veritas, Vita,' The Way, The Truth and the Life.' What a glorious opportunity to tell of Jesus, the way, the truth and the life.

Jesus said to him, "I am the way, the truth, and the life. No one comes to the Father except through Me". John 14:6

Spirituality and Faith in the Treatment of Substance Misuse

*if My people who are called by My name will humble themselves, and
pray and seek My face, and turn from their wicked ways, then I will
hear from heaven, and will forgive their sin and heal their land*
2 Chronicles 7:14

This chapter contains a special study presented as a part of the
requirement for the degree of Master of Arts Theology and Religious
Studies (April 2011). As people who believe in the God of hope we
started hearing stories of the huge failure rates in standard
rehabilitation centres, but we also heard of a significantly higher
success rate in Christian rehabilitation centres. This chapter relates my
findings in which the amazing truth of how tackling the spiritual
dimension behind addictions is the key to breaking the habits of a
lifetime and living a new life in Jesus.

Introduction

In this paper I intend looking at drug treatment today, the issues of the
rehabilitation of drug addicts and what part spirituality and faith have
in the success of treatment. Currently there are an estimated 320,000
problem drug users in England alone.[1] This has created a vast problem,
not just for the users themselves, but for the National Health Service
in providing clinical and medical support, for Local Authorities in
providing housing and social services, for the Police in public order and
criminal activity and for society in general.

---

[1] The National Drug and Alcoholism Treatment Unit Survey 2009-10.

During my research I focussed on three drug treatment centres. I visited The Haven Residential Centre[2] in Kilmacolm and the Glasgow Drugs Crisis Centre[3]. I also used the website of Phoenix Futures to access information about their residential unit in Glasgow. All information gathered from these three units is freely available in the public domain by accessing their websites.

The perception in society is that 'once an addict always an addict'. I will be looking at the reality of this statement and in what way government policy seems to validate it.

My interest in this subject comes from my time as a voluntary worker in a Christian outreach centre, where we serve drug addicts, alcoholics, the homeless and anybody in need, a hot meal on a Sunday. Whilst working there I heard the claim that when it comes to drug treatment and drug rehabilitation, faith based organisations have a far better 'success' rate than government programmes. The statistic I was quoted was that faith based programs had a success rate of around 80% when it came to drug rehabilitation compared to an 8% success rate for non-faith based programmes. This intrigued me and I decided to research where these figures come from and, if accurate, what it is that makes such a huge difference.

My initial intention was to look at alcoholics and drug addicts and study them in residential settings. However, as my research shows, inpatient care for alcoholics is only deemed necessary in the most extreme of cases and now for drug addicts the use of residential care is also becoming a very low percentage of treatment offered, as low as 2% [4]. I will be looking at the thinking behind this, and also looking at what has now become the focus for treatment today.

I will be looking at the treatment of substance abusers and how we perceive and approach treatment of these problems. I am particularly interested in the rehabilitation process as opposed to the detoxification process. Detoxification is classed as 'Humane

---

[2] ER 23. www.thehavenkilmacolm.com
[3] ER 21. http://www.turningpointscotland.com/services/glasgow_drug_crisis_centre
[4] ER1. http://www.bbc.co.uk/blogs/thereporters/markeaston/2008/10/drug_treatment_officials_were.html

withdrawal from a drug of dependence'[5] while Rehabilitation is seen as being 'Long-term abstinence and re-integration into society'[6].

I will be looking at the 'harm reduction program'[7] and its more widely accepted use for treatment compared to the use of rehabilitation programs. I will be looking at what they do in this harm reduction programme and what results they are looking for. Finally, I will be looking at residential rehabilitation care and what it provides. At this point I will be comparing the success figures for faith based and for secular centres.

In my research I found that while there are private rehabilitation centres, many are run by charities, supported to a greater or lesser degree by government funding. These centres are all run by dedicated people. In general, I found three types of rehabilitation centre;, those which are run by people of faith and base their program around their beliefs, those which are run by people of faith but focus on the faith side of things in a very limited way and those who avoid religious overtones of any kind. It has to be said that the term 'spiritual' is used widely in treatment provision but usually there is an avoidance of any kind of religious connotation unless it is a faith based organisation which is running the program.

My reading will include areas of research by government, medical and sociology bodies. The topic I am covering has a wide range of interest groups from Social Services, the National Health Service, the Police, and the public at large. Many factors are involved in why people, aside from the addicts themselves, have a problem with substance misuse. There is the anti-social behaviour it can cause, there is the criminal element, and there is the health factor. Family, friends and society in general, can all be affected in some way by the substance misusers.

Part of my research has been deductive in nature in that having a general conclusion of the success rate of faith based over non-faith based I have set out to look for data to back this up. As will be seen one

---

[5] ER 13. www.scotland.gov.uk/resource/doc/180429 *Review of Residential Drug Detoxification and Rehabilitation Services in Scotland.*
[6] ER 13. www.scotland.gov.uk/resource/doc/180429 *Review of Residential Drug Detoxification and Rehabilitation Services in Scotland.*
[7] Reducing Drug-Related Harm: An Action Plan (DH & NTA, 2007):

of the main problems I came across was in defining 'success'. The definition of success, as we will see, can vary considerably, from being able to stabilise the chaotic lifestyle of the substance abuser to their complete abstinence.

I then looked at the methodology of rehabilitation centres. I looked to ascertain if there was any difference in the methods used, or are they basically the same? What, if anything, makes the difference? Is it the faith of the staff? Or Is it the faith of the person attending the rehab?

I looked at the rehabilitation (as opposed to detoxification) of people addicted to alcohol and drugs. In particular I am interested in looking at the success rate of residential rehabilitation clinics and comparing the success rates of faith based and secular rehabilitation centres.

Substance Abuse in Today's Society

Substance abuse, or substance misuse, is a big problem in today's society however as Luke Bretherton puts it, 'Trying to find theological reflection on drug use is like trying to find an unprofitable drug dealer'[8]. I found that most of the writings I came across were either from the departments of medicine or sociology, or government sources. Drug use is not a new phenomenon in the history of man, but I am going to look at the increased use of a chemical solution to life since the 1960's. Leech states that 'Our drug orientated culture has assumed that there is a chemical solution to all human problems.'[9] Leech goes on to quote figures for the increase in prescribed medications 'Between 1965 and 1970 in Britain there was a 220 percent increase in medical prescribing of minor tranquilisers. By 1970 47.2 million prescriptions for psychotropic or mood altering drugs were issued in England and Wales alone, amounting to some 3,000 million pills.'[10] This attitude from the medical world, that moods can be controlled by drugs, became prevalent in our social lives. A wide range of drugs became available in addition to the already widely available

---

[8] Bretherton, Luke.2008. In *Public Theology in Cultural Engagement*. Milton Keynes: Paternoster. P.94.

[9] Leech, Kenneth.1992. *The Eye of The Storm*. Cambridge: University Press. P.8.

[10] Peter, Parish. in *Drugs and Society 7:1 (April 1972)* P.12.

drug of alcohol. Drugs themselves are not the problem, but it is our use of them, driven by our desire for maximum pleasure for minimal effort 'If what causes problems with drugs is not initially or primarily the drugs themselves but our sinful characters, then we must learn how to manage our responses to drugs in the light of our fallen condition. Managing our responses to drugs means undertaking to school the flesh and avoid establishing patterns of life (either corporately or individually) that encourages dependency on drugs.' [11]

Lifestyle is what drives our choices and therefore lifestyle changes will inevitably be the solution to our drug habits. Simply attempting abstinence will not see a permanent solution. Part of the substance abuse problem is driven by our consumer society, we are taught that the more we consume the more successful we must be, more cars, more clothes, more food, more pleasure, and pleasure in a materialistic society has to be bought and consumed. In his novel *Generation X,* Douglas Coupland [12] has a poignant scene in which a group of twenty-somethings try to remember a precious moment from childhood that does not involve a commercialised, consumer experience. They succeed, but only just [13]. Our place in a materialistic society is related to our ability to consume Bretherton says, 'In contemporary Western societies, one of the primary modes of involvement in society is as a consumer, rather than, say, an agriculturalist, warrior or hunter-gatherer' [14].

We are no longer what we do, but what we consume, in that the more you consume the more worth you feel you have. In many ways the search for fulfilment in chemicals comes from the scientific presumption that we are merely a collection of chemicals, and when these chemicals are in perfect balance then we will be in perfect harmony with all around us. However, so far no one has been able to come up with the perfect, permanent chemical solution and the chemicals we use to give us pleasure are at best fleeting in their

[11] Bretherton, Luke.2008. In *Public Theology in Cultural Engagement*. Milton Keynes: Paternoster. P124.

[12] Coupland, Douglas. 1991. *Generation X: Tales of an Accelerated Culture.* New York: St. Martin's. p.87-96.

[13] Bretherton, Luke. 2008. In *Public Theology in Cultural Engagement*. Milton Keynes: Paternoster. P.107.

[14] Ibis. P.106.

success. Christianity, and indeed most other faiths, believes that human beings are not just a collection of chemicals but also have a spiritual dimension to them. Religion points to a spiritual dimension to the human being and therefore addressing the chemical imbalance in our bodies, while important, will never fully satisfy our search for fulfilment. What I will be looking at later is the question, 'does introducing a spiritual element to recovery programs bring an increase in success rates?'

Alcohol misuse is by far the most socially acceptable form of substance misuse. The use of alcohol is often seen as the behavioural norm; in today's society it is deemed that it becomes a problem only for the very few. However, this view of alcohol and the problems it produces is changing. 80% of people think that more should be done to tackle the level of alcohol abuse in society [15]. However, the term 'in society' can be very misleading and can hinder the individual from seeing alcohol abuse as an individual's problem and focus it as being 'society's problem'. Most people's perception of alcohol being a problem is not in terms of their own usage or the harm it does to them, but in terms of the social disturbance at a weekend, or at social gatherings where drink is involved, such as football matches, night clubs or music festivals. In the Government's booklet on this subject *Safe. Sensible. Social. The Next Steps in the National Alcohol Strategy,* their focus is to provide three things:

1. Tackling alcohol-fuelled crime and disorder.

2. Focus on the minority of drinkers who cause harm to themselves and society.

3. Actively promote sensible drinking.

In this type of environment, where alcohol is seen as socially acceptable and the focus is in making it more socially acceptable, the person who has a problem with alcohol will struggle to deal with it and it will take longer to diagnose alcohol abuse and suggest treatment. Alcohol misuse is seen as less of a problem than drug misuse. I have been in environments where the behaviour of the people taking alcohol was no different than the perceived behaviour of drug users.

---

[15] Department of Health. *Safe. Sensible. Social. The Next Steps in the National Alcohol Strategy.* P.5.

Drinking till they are incapacitated, falling asleep where they sit and then waking up and drinking more, this cycle could continue for days yet the drinker would still turn up their nose if a drug addict appeared at the party. Drug abusers are perceived to be untrustworthy and will rob you as soon as look at you. 'In the Glasgow area in 2005-06, 2,923 people were arrested for drunkenness, while there were 14,238 drug related arrests.' [16]

This would seem to indicate that people high on drugs are more likely to behave socially unacceptably than people who are drunk. There are no statistics available that can tell if offences (such as house breaking) have been committed to support a drug habit. The Beckley Report (March 2009) states that '14.4% of the Scottish prison population are drug offenders' [17]. A further report on Perth prison states that 28% of inmates tested positive for drugs. Chief Inspector of Prisons, Brigadier Hugh Munro said at 28%, the figure was "far too high" and suggested drugs were being smuggled into the jail [18]. Both figures, however, represent a minority in overall terms of inmates therefore the perception by alcoholics that drug addicts are the reason for all crime and socially unacceptable behaviour would seem to be incorrect.

What does society prescribe for an alcoholic recovering?

In most instances residential rehabilitation is not offered. During my research I became aware that treatment recommendations for alcohol misuse and drug misuse were different. 'Reflecting the usual mild nature of the withdrawal syndrome, many public administrators have opted to establish a series of levels of care, ranging from outpatient to 'social-model' detoxification facilities to inpatient care, when needed.'[19]

---

[16] ER 2. P.62 http://www.drugmisuse.isdscotland.org/dat/cap/2007_08/Greater%20Glasgow%20and%20Clyde%20.pdf

[17] ER 3. P.4. http://www.idpc.net/phpbin/documents/Beckley_Report_16_2_FINAL_EN.pdf

[18] ER 4. http://news.bbc.co.uk/1/hi/scotland/tayside_and_central/8618199.stm

[19] Schuckit,Mark. 2006. *Drug and Alcohol Abuse, A Clinical Guide to Diagnosis and Treatment*. New York: Springer: P.123.

The twelve-step program was initiated by Alcoholics Anonymous and is now a common feature in most recovery programs.

'A survey of 450 treatment centres found that 93 percent used the Twelve-Step philosophy. Other estimates put it lower, at 80 percent, but H. Wesley Clark, director of the Federal Centre for Substance abuse Treatment, said the figure was definitely in the range between the two.' [20]

These programs are not, in general, inpatient programs. The twelve steps include the involvement of a higher power, and you are left to make of that what you will, but the program as well as supplying a high level of support and accountability has an element of the spiritual; the laying down of your chemical solution and submitting to a spiritual solution. All twelve steps in the program contain a spiritual element, from the more obvious of submitting to God (as we understood him), to aspects of spirituality in confession and reconciliation. These are the original Twelve Steps as published by Alcoholics Anonymous. (I have underlined all those parts with a religious or spiritual aspect to them.)

1. We admitted we were powerless over alcohol-that our lives had become unmanageable. (Confession)

2. Came to believe that a Power greater than ourselves could restore us to sanity.

3. Made a decision to turn our will and our lives over to the care of God *as we understood Him.*

4. Made a searching and fearless moral inventory of ourselves.

5. Admitted to God, to ourselves, and to another human being the exact nature of our wrongs.

6. Were entirely ready to have God remove all these defects of character.

7. Humbly asked Him to remove our shortcomings.

8. Made a list of all persons we had harmed, and became willing to make amends to them all. (Reconciliation)

---

[20] Ringwald, Christopher D. 2002. *The Soul Of Recovery.* New York: Oxford University Press. P.4.

9. Made direct amends to such people wherever possible, except when to do so would injure them or others. (Reconciliation)

10. Continued to take personal inventory and when we were wrong promptly admitted it. (Self-examination)

11. Sought through prayer and meditation to improve our conscious contact with God *as we understood Him,* praying only for knowledge of His will for us and the power to carry that out.

12. Having had a spiritual awakening as the result of these steps, we tried to carry this message to alcoholics, and to practice these principles in all our affairs. [21]

When I was originally looking at my topic, I wanted to look at drug and alcohol rehabilitation within a residential setting. My reading has suggested that the rehabilitation of alcoholics in a residential setting is not appropriate. Primarily, it has to be said, from a cost point of view. It has been estimated that outpatient services account for 87% of all clients [22]. The main objection to inpatient care for alcohol abuse is cost; Stockwell (1987) concludes that:

'home detoxification with supervised medication is as effective and safe, among the patients for whom it is suitable, as inpatient care' [23]. Hayadisha et al. (1989)[24] compared the effectiveness and costs of inpatient and outpatient detoxification for problem drinkers with mild-to-moderate withdrawal symptoms. They found no difference in effectiveness between the two, but the inpatient programme was over ten times more expensive [25].

The cost of private residential rehabilitation clinics is prohibitive to all but the most well off. Most clinics do not advertise their price structure, but I found these two indicative prices ranges: Lifeworks Community, Surrey, inpatient care, £650 per day, with a minimum of

---

[21] ER 5. http://www.aa.org/en_pdfs/smf-121_en.pdf

[22] Jung, John. 2010. *Alcohol, other Drugs, and Behaviour.* P.379.

[23] Stockwell T., & Clement S., Eds. 1987. H*elping the Problem Drinker: Newlinitiatives in Community Care.* London: Croom Helm.

[24] Hayashida m et al, *Article in New England Journal o fMedicine.* 320: 358-365 1989

[25] Heather, Nick.1995 *Treatment Approaches to Alcohol Problems.* P.17.

7 days, [26] Perry Clayman Project, Luton and Chelmsford, 2 week program £2,495, 12 week program £6,950 [27]. Needless to say, government treatment programs are very reluctant to use rehabilitation clinics. Faith based centres offer the general public a cheap alternative, but do they work?

I do voluntary work with people who have substance abuse problems, some with alcohol, some with drugs, some with both. I observed a problem with them often continually in and out of one program or another, including prison, and rehabilitation centres. The fact that they seemed to continually revert to their old habits, including drug use, concerned me, and I became interested in residential rehabilitation centres.

On hearing the statistic of an 80% success rate for faith based programmes and only 8% for secular programmes I was intrigued and wanted to find out more. This was not just a small difference but a major difference. But was it valid or just wishful thinking?

I found that the statistic I had been quoted comes from an early study in 1976 by the National Institute on Drug Abuse, [28] an American based organisation, however it is still being quoted today on Teen challenge's website. Sherman (2003) in her paper quoted this figure saying, 'that an astonishing 86 Percent of Teen Challenge graduates remained drug free seven years after their graduation from the program' [29].

Sherman's study was based on a program run by Teen Challenge [30]; a Christian organisation coming under the Assemblies of God denomination, it originates in America but is now in 82 countries worldwide. Often promoted as a drug rehabilitation organisation its overtly Christian teachings are a concern for an increasingly secular society. However, the mission statement of Teen Challenge reads:

'To provide youth, adults and families with an effective and comprehensive Christian faith-based solution to life-controlling drug

---

[26] ER 6. www.lifeworkscommunity.com

[27] ER 7. www.rehabtoday.com

[28] ER 8. http://www.nida.nih.gov/nidahome.html

[29] Sherman, Amy L., 2003. *Faith in Communities: A Solid Investment*. Society, January/February 2003. P.5.

[30] ER 9. http://www.teenchallenge.org.uk/

and alcohol problems in order to become productive members of society. By applying biblical principles, Teen Challenge endeavours to help people become mentally-sound, emotionally-balanced, socially-adjusted, physically-well, and spiritually-alive.' [31]

Their openly Christian message and teachings are part of their overall mission statement and people entering their program are made aware of this. However, society's aversion to Christians proselytising means they are continually under scrutiny, particularly when people are placed on the program as part of the criminal justice system, since agreeing to partake in the program can be a way of avoiding incarceration. People placed in drug rehabilitation programs by the justice system do surprisingly well. 'Successful clients were more likely to have been admitted on an involuntary basis, as a condition of probation or parole, or with criminal charges pending. This finding was unexpected in view of the usual assumption that clients who seek treatment on a voluntary basis have a higher level of motivation, leading to greater treatment success.' [32]

In America, 23% of people on Teen Challenge's drug rehabilitation programme are referred to them by a court, and a further 7% are referred by some other social services department [33]. For publicly funded programs, there is a core problem in the data collected to assess treatment effectiveness. Up to the present time, it has not been of a uniform nature, which prevents accurate assessments about program effectiveness.

The following exchange in 1992 on the effectiveness of federally-funded treatment programs between Mark V. Nadel, the General Accounting Office's Associate Director for National and Public Health Issues (US), and Charles B. Rangel, then Chairman of the Select Committee on Narcotics Abuse and Control in the House of Representatives (US), illustrates the severity of the problem:

---

[31] ER 10. http://teenchallengeusa.com/about/

[32] Sidwall, James W, Conway, Gail L.1998. in *The International Journal of the Addictions, 23(12), 1241-1254,*1988 P.1251.

[33] A Review of a Study by Dr. Aaron T. Bicknese *"The Teen Challenge Drug Treatment Program in Comparative Perspective"* 1999.

Mr. Nadel: As we found in our report, because uniform information is not being collected, we are unable to provide you with that information.

Mr. Rangel: How can we compare the success of one [type of treatment] to another?

Mr. Nadel: If you had good uniform data and outcome data on a continuing basis, you would be able to do so. We don't have such data now.

Mr. Rangel: So, you haven't the slightest idea as to whether any of these treatments are working?

Mr. Nadel: We are unable to determine that. That's right, Mr. Chairman.[34]

It would seem remarkable that government departments have no way of determining the effectiveness of government run programmes for the treatment of substance abuse. The latest U.S. Government statistics are now 18 years old.

'The NDATUS [35] data are no longer up to date, but the 1992 findings provide a baseline measure.' [36]

Due to the variables in how to judge the success of a program or otherwise there is no new coherent data available on this issue. Most statistics are based on how many are on the program and not how successful the program is. Many people start programmes but do not complete them. The main problem is how success is defined. Governments tend to use the figure most beneficial for their cause, as can be seen in a recent study of the UK Government statistics. Here Easton finds that the actual percentage of people successfully rehabilitated from drugs in government based programs was 3.6%.

---

[34] United States House of Representatives, Select Committee on Narcotics Abuse and Control, Drug Abuse
Treatment: A Review of Current Federal Programs and Policies: Hearing, 102nd Congress, 1st session
(Washington, D.C.: Government Printing Office, 1992), pp. 73-74.
[35] The National Drug and Alcoholism Treatment Unit Survey.
[36] Jung, John. 2010. *Alcohol, other Drugs, and Behaviour.* P.379.

'The National Treatment Agency (NTA) yesterday published its annual figures showing yet another big increase in the numbers of people who were on the drug treatment programme last year - 202,000 altogether. Not mentioned in the press notice, discretely lodged in a table near the bottom of the data release, was the number of people who left the treatment programme drug-free last year - 7,324. What I did, and what so infuriated the people at the NTA, was to compare the two. The arithmetic was pretty simple. Just 3.6% of those in treatment were discharged free of illegal drugs. The system had been patting itself on the back for getting lots of people signed up for treatment but people had not noticed what happened afterwards. The focus was on inputs not outcomes. In a report sent to drug teams this week, the NTA itself bemoans the way that residential services are too often used as a last resort rather than as a concerted attempt to achieve long-term abstinence earlier in a drug-using career.' [37]

The use of residential services is costly and unproven, due to the way statistics are gathered, however Teen Challenge claims of a 70% cure rate for the drug addicts graduating from their program attracted the attention of the U.S. Federal Government in 1973. Most secular drug rehabilitation programs only experienced a cure rate of 1-15% of their graduates. The National Institute on Drug Abuse (NIDA), part of the U.S. Department of Health, Education, and Welfare, funded the first year of this study to evaluate the long term results of the Teen Challenge program. [38]

A follow-up study in 1994 of Teen Challenge graduates found that '67 percent of those who graduated were continuing to abstain from drug and alcohol use' [39].

The key word here I find to be 'graduate', the figures do not take into account the dropout rate, which can be almost 50%. To graduate, the drug addict will have to have gone through a 12 to 18 month program and be fully indoctrinated into Christianity. Completion of this program should in itself promote a better choice of lifestyle, but even in non-

---

[37] ER 1. http://www.bbc.co.uk/blogs/thereporters/markeaston/2008/10/drug_treatment_officials_were.html

[38] ER 11. http://www.acadc.org/page/page/2495014.htm

[39] Sherman, Amy L., *Faith in Communities: A Solid Investment*. Society, January/February 2003 p.5.

faith based rehabilitation centres if they are inclusive and give the person a feeling of being part of something bigger than themselves then this too can lead to continuing abstinence as shown in the 12 step program promoted by Alcoholics Anonymous. This style of recovery is based on focusing on something or someone bigger than you and on accountability to a mentor.

The reason behind wanting to get free from addiction has to be greater than the pull of the addiction. The pull of the addiction is not just the drug but has many social factors as well. That's where I believe Christian rehabilitation centres could have an edge. They have something bigger than the addiction to offer, they have a social structure, the church, to feed people into after rehabilitation and they can give them a support system based on acceptance and love. This is acknowledged by Teen Challenge and again is a pointer to their success rates, the follow up and inclusion in a community is important

'Upon graduation, students are made aware of educational and ministry opportunities in their local community colleges and churches. Although pursuing higher education has obvious benefits for any individual, it is vital that the Church has a place for those in the aftercare process. Continuing involvement in the local church is critical to the on-going development of any believer, especially those who have come through the battleground of addiction.' [40]

For many addicts, returning to the community they came from after rehabilitation means returning to old friends and even family who may still be using drugs. The follow up and the support system has to be as good as the rehabilitation program, otherwise the chance of going back to old habits is very high. A rehabilitation program without a continuing support system becomes just a detoxification program where the person becomes substance free but is very likely to re-offend.

'Common sense dictates that the most thorough physical examination, the best opportunity for close observation, and the largest number of

---

[40] ER 12. http://teenchallengeusa.com/program/

treatment options are provided by supervision of withdrawal in an inpatient treatment setting.' [41]

The most successful detoxification program is run by HM Prison services; however this seldom involves successful rehabilitation. The rehabilitation back up from social service is there but they are often regarded as a parole officer rather than a support system and viewed with suspicion. The biggest problem is how the addict, now cleaned up, copes with being returned to the area they left.

'The transition back into the wider community (especially when living alone) is difficult to achieve despite preparation for leaving being incorporated into the program. The problems inherent in separation are rarely managed successfully even with those individuals who stabilize, develop and thrive in the community setting.' [42]

In my own research I came across M. who after 9 years on drugs ended up in jail, went through the detoxification program and came out clean, and well fed. The services and support were there but on his release, he didn't go to his appointment with his housing officer, didn't want to go to bed and breakfast because he had two dogs, and he was immediately back with his own crowd of drinkers and drug abusers, sleeping wherever he could. It took him and a friend several weeks to get a flat. His friend, a drug addict has since died; but M. still doesn't use the support services available. At the moment he says he is off of drugs, but he still drinks. These people are very self-reliant and that can be a big problem, since to overcome addictions requires a supportive community and accountability.

'Successful program completion was also associated with family participation in treatment and the development of a social support system.' [43]

Current Treatment Methods

---

[41] Schuckit, Marc A. 2006. *Drug and Alcohol Abuse. A Clinical Guide to Diagnosis and Treatment 6th edition.* New York: Springer. P.123.

[42] Elliott, Barbara, 2003. *Containing the Uncontainable.* p.13.

[43] Sidwall,James W, Conway, Gail L.1998. in *The International Journal of the Addictions, 23(12), 1241-1254,*1988 P.1252.

Very few drug addicts are in residential rehabilitation care, research shows that the overwhelming majority of people being treated for drug abuse are in fact being treated in the community.

'A very small proportion are in rehab. The latest figures show that 147,000 of the individuals in treatment were being given prescribed medication - 74% of all those on the programme. How many accessed residential rehab? The data shows it was less than 5,000 - around 2% of the treatment population.' [44]

This leads to the Government being able to produce more positive looking statistics; however, while the statistics look better, having people in treatment is not, as we shall see, the same as offering people a chance to be drug free.

'The NTA [45] prefer to focus on the number in treatment and the number retained for 12 weeks - the government's measures of success. There is no target for getting people off drugs' [46]

There are many ways in which the Government are trying to tackle the drug problem, residential services being just one of them

'A total of £9.08 million was spent on residential detoxification and rehabilitation Services in 2005-6. Of this, 68% (£6.1m) came from local authority budgets while 32% (£2.9m) came from NHS Boards.' [47] (These figures are for Scotland.)

Residential rehabilitation is expensive and with Government success rates at around 11% [48] it is very hard to justify funding, therefore the Government has been focusing on moving away from residential care

---

[44] ER 1. http://www.bbc.co.uk/blogs/thereporters/markeaston/2008/10/drug_treatment_officials_were.html

[45] The National Treatment Agency (NTA)

[46] ER 1. http://www.bbc.co.uk/blogs/thereporters/markeaston/2008/10/drug_treatment_officials_were.html

[47] ER 13. www.scotland.gov.uk/resource/doc/180429 *Review of Residential Drug Detoxification and Rehabilitation Services in Scotland.*

[48] ER 14. http://www.nta.nhs.uk/facts.aspx

towards care in the community. Outpatient treatment has been the prevailing mode since the early to mid 1990s [49].

The only figures available for successful rehabilitation of any kind in significant numbers are in faith based programs, yet these are closing down due to lack of government funding.

'Since 1975 the Church of Scotland's social care arm CrossReach has run the Argyll-based Ronachan House, and it is with a heavy heart the organisation decided to close it because drastically low referral numbers from local authorities made it financially unviable. Its final day was Friday 3rd December 2010.' [50]

So why should the Government place people in faith based residential centres, the short answer is they appear to be working. The Governments main focus in treating drug addicts does not centre around abstinence and rehabilitation, whether as an inpatient or an outpatient, but now focuses on what is referred to as 'harm reduction programs'. The official definition for this term is:

'Harm reduction combines work aimed directly at reducing the number of drug related deaths and blood borne virus infections, with wider goals of preventing drug misuse and of encouraging stabilisation in treatment and support for abstinence. Providing effective substitution treatments and effective support for abstinence are complementary aims of such a balanced response' [51]

This definition contains the term 'support for abstinence'; there are no figures that show providing needles and supplying Methadone actually help in producing abstinence.

The needle exchange program was first introduced in the UK in 1985 and is for the provision of clean needles to injecting addicts who would otherwise share needles and risk cross contamination of diseases such as HIV and Hepatitis C. In 2005-06 a total of 502,159 needles were supplied in the Greater Glasgow area alone [52]. This is part

---

[49] Christopher D. Ringwald, *The Soul Of Recovery*. (New York: Oxford University Press, 2002),.11.
[50] ER 24. http://www.crossreach.org.uk/node/178
[51] Reducing Drug-Related Harm: An Action Plan (DH & NTA, 2007):
[52] ER 2. P.47. http://www.drugmisuse.isdscotland.org/dat/cap/2007_08/

of the 'harm reduction program' and has no proven value as either a detoxification method or a step towards rehabilitation. There is however a perceived benefit to the community at large

'While NSPs (needle and syringe programmes) can help reduce the harm caused to people who inject drugs, the consequent reduction in the prevalence of blood-borne viruses benefits wider society.' [53]

As well as the needle exchange program which supports people who want to continue using drugs, albeit in a safer environment, the Government also supply Methadone to those wishing to stop using Heroin. Methadone is used as an opiate substitute particularly for heroin and is only available through prescription.

'In 2005-06 in Greater Glasgow Area there were 8,954 people on Methadone.' [54]

It is used to stabilise people from the withdrawal effects when trying to come of Opiates.

'Methadone is an opiate drug that is the most widely used drug treatment for opiate dependence (National Consensus Development Panel, 1998).' [55]

Higher doses of methadone can block the euphoric effects of heroin, morphine, and similar drugs. As a result, properly dosed methadone patients can reduce or stop altogether their use of these substances; however they remain on Methadone. Methadone tends to be used more as a stabilizing drug, prior to or as part of a detoxification program. While a recent study by Edinburgh University showed Methadone as having a stabilizing effect on drug users it is harder to see any significant abstinence resulting from its use

'This study confirms that methadone works and works best when prescribed for as long as is needed. Even though some users continue to occasionally inject while on methadone, they still gain substantial

---

Greater%20Glasgow%20and%20Clyde%20.pdf
[53] National Institute for Health and Clinical Excellence (2009, February), 'Needle and syringe programmes: Guidance'
[54] ER 2. P.127.http://www.drugmisuse.isdscotland.org/dat/cap/2007_08/ Greater%20Glasgow%20and%20Clyde%20.pdf
[55] ER 15. http://priory.com/psychiatry/Methadone.htm *Dr Jason Luty et al*

health benefits from their prescription. Suggestions that methadone prescribing should be cut back or used in the short-term are clearly misplaced and would lead to poorer health for drug injectors.' [56]

As can be seen from the results of this study published in the British Medical Journal (July 2010) [57] the use of Methadone has no apparent value in rehabilitating the drug user

Conclusions

Opiate substitution treatment in injecting drug users in primary care reduces this risk of mortality, with survival benefits increasing with cumulative exposure to treatment. <u>Treatment does not reduce the overall duration of injecting.</u> [58]

The use of Methadone is part of the harm reduction program where the risk of death and illness is reduced, and the drug user is able to lead a less chaotic lifestyle; this benefits society at large by the drug user being perceived as less likely to be disruptive to society. There is, however, a call for more productive methods to be used rather than being satisfied with harm reduction programmes

'Its use has been criticised by Scottish Conservatives, who claimed addicts are "parked" on methadone. The party has called for the underlying causes of abuse to be tackled, and for more addicts to be put into rehabilitation programmes, including in prisons.' [59]

However, the idea of putting people in prison where they will be part of a rehabilitation program would require a change of policy by the Government who have now introduced the dispensing of Methadone to inmates in prisons on a large scale

---

[56] ER 16. http://www.ed.ac.uk/news/all-news/methadone-080710 *Dr Roy Roberston, Honorary Clinical reader, centre for population health services*
[57] Survival and cessation in injecting drug users: prospective observational study of outcomes and effect of opiate substitution treatment BMJ 2010; 341:c3172
[58] ER 17. http://www.bmj.com/content/341/bmj.c3172.full *Matthew Hickman, professor in public health and epidemiology from Department of Social Medicine, University of Bristol, Bristol BS8 2PS.*
[59] ER 18. http://www.bbc.co.uk/news/10558740

'last year a record 20,000 English prisoners were prescribed the addictive heroin substitute methadone instead of being encouraged to use their time inside to get drug-free.' [60]

This represents approximately one third of the prison population in England. Prisons use Methadone as a way of keeping addicts subdued; they do not have any program which uses Methadone as an effective detoxification and rehabilitation tool.

Noreen Oliver who runs the Burton Addiction Centre believes voters would be shocked by how few prisoners are given the chance to get off drugs: "I think what the public wants is their money getting people off drugs, back contributing to society and out of the benefits system. At the moment that's only happening for 850 prisoners out of 60,000 who are actually given the chance to become drug-free."[61] However, the use of Methadone is a recognised method of dealing with prisoners who otherwise may have to go through 'cold turkey' on entering prison which can be distressing and even life threatening to the addict.

'The provision of methadone in prisons is considered best practice by the World Health Organisation, the UN Office on Drugs and Crime, and UNAIDS', among other esteemed national and international expert bodies.' [62]

Glasgow Drug Crisis Centre

In March 2011 I attended an open event at Glasgow Drugs Crisis Centre [63] (situated just over the river from the city centre); the event was open to students and professionals with an interest in drug rehabilitation services. It is run by Turning Point Scotland [64], a registered charity. Their stated aim is

---

[60] ER 19. http://www.bbc.co.uk/blogs/thereporters/markeaston/2009/12/a_substitute_for_prison_drugs.html
[61] ER 19. http://www.bbc.co.uk/blogs/thereporters/markeaston/2009/12/a_substitute_for_prison_drugs.html
[62] ER 20.http://www.timesonline.co.uk/tol/comment/letters/article6955116.ece *Professor Gerry Stimson Executive Director, International Harm Reduction Association.*
[63] ER 21. http://www.turningpointscotland.com/services/glasgow_drug_crisis_centre
[64] ER 22. http://www.turningpointscotland.com/

'Glasgow Drug Crisis Centre (GDCC) offers a safe, confidential service which will support and encourage people to find ways for making their substance misuse less problematic and to achieve a better quality of life. Supporting people in their own recovery journeys, everyone who attends GDCC can have an initial assessment of their circumstances completed and holistic care plan drawn up. Individuals can obtain advice about community-based organizations that can provide longer term support and care management throughout their own personal recovery journey.' [65]

In line with the prevailing thoughts and policies on drug treatment the services they provide are focused on 'harm reduction' rather than abstinence. They can supply all the kit you need to safely inject, including needles (various sizes), filters, lemon juice, spoons, swabs, everything but the drug. For clients who are sexually active they also provide condoms. Clients are anonymous and are expected to supply a dirty needle in exchange for a clean one. They are not allowed to inject on the premises, however one member of staff expressed a desire to have this allowed. His argument was that in the last three years six addicts had left their premises and overdosed within a few hundred yards. Had they injected on the premises the staff would have been able to stabilise them and have them admitted to Accident & Emergency. Staff members are trained in the administration of Naloxone which reduces the risk of fatality in the event of overdose, the centre also provides training to addicts on the safe self-administration of Naloxone. We must never forget that we are dealing with life and death issues. Each human life is important and harm reduction is primarily focusing on keeping these people alive with the hope that one day they will have the desire to change. The first step in all rehabilitation is the individual's desire to change.

The Centre also has a nurse on hand to supply Methadone; however the unit cannot supply Methadone to clients unless they have a prescription. A Doctor is available every morning to see patients and prescribe medication and give a general health check. They also provide a special abscess and ulcer clinic.

---

[65] ER 21. http://www.turningpointscotland.com/services/glasgow_drug_crisis_centre

At the Drug Crisis Centre they have a twelve bed residential unit but clients can only use this for a maximum of twenty one days while they are stabilized, it is not used as a rehabilitation unit. It is aimed at clients who are no longer coping in the community, however while in the residential unit they are offered varied support with issues in their lives such as assistance with court cases, housing, health problems, family issues and anything that may be concerning them. The staff here do use the opportunity to assist the client to assess their lifestyle and perhaps consider doing something more permanent about their habit. If the client wishes they will assist them to enter residential care, but it very much has to be client driven. At the end of the day the value of harm reduction programs cannot be dismissed because people are not drug free at the end of them, some people may never be drug free, but they do deserve the chance to have less chaotic lives and an opportunity at life itself. In drug treatment you are dealing with life or death issues every day.

While the Drug Crisis Centre is a focal point for addicts who are desperate, needle exchange programs and Methadone are also supplied from many local chemists. There is also a multitude of in-community rehabilitation and detoxification programs; the drug problem is not getting any smaller. For in community treatment the cost per person is relatively small compared to the cost of residential rehabilitation

'The average cost spent per person for residential treatment is £20,000 compared to that of £3,000 for treatment in the community. Residential programs have a dropout rate of 33%, and for 28% of people entering residential treatment it will not be their first time.' [66]

However, the aim of residential care is quite explicit, to give the client an environment where he can become drug free and remain so after leaving the unit. Of the few who do get into residential units, how are they going to be successful and why do we see such variances in the success rate claims between faith based and secular treatment centres? 70% compared to 3.6%. What differences are there in the regimes themselves? And can someone with no faith be successful in a

---

[66] ER 13. www.scotland.gov.uk/resource/doc/180429 *Review of Residential Drug Detoxification and Rehabilitation Services in Scotland.*

faith based program? Is a drug free life a possibility? When society and government programs give up on them who will care?

Residential Rehabilitation Centres

The cost of inpatient treatment is one of the main concerns when it comes to treating drug addicts. Many of the residential centres are private, particularly for alcohol abuse, and are therefore funded by the patient themselves. However, when it comes to Government funding these residential centres have to come up with results: in England the government has introduced Payment by Results (PbR) [67]. With the need for cuts in budgets throughout the health industry what funds are available have to be targeted where the most efficient use of funds can be proven. Unfortunately, these are the factors that are going to determine what type of treatment is going to be available to patients, not just drug addicts but throughout the healthcare system. As Karen Briggs chief executive of Phoenix Futures said to the recent Drugscope Annual Conference in November 2010:

'As much as we might hate it, we need to justify why we should exist and play to whatever agenda it takes to protect the funding we need to deliver what we know works. Payment by results is a feature of our future. Much of the detail is yet to be announced but what is clear is that it will radically change the landscape of drug and alcohol treatment over the coming years.' [68]

Potential costs for each person successfully rehabilitated

One of the residential centres I looked at, The Haven in Kilmacolm is considered successful. It claims to have a relatively high success rate of 50%. But here again we have the problem of what is success? And who is counting? The figure I was quoted was just an estimate from one of the trustees. But if we were to take it as accurate, we have to put it into the context of a 12 bed unit with a further 6 beds in the halfway house. As the programme is designed to last 12 to 15 months, nine months in the main unit with a further six months in the halfway house, it would mean that if the unit was running at maximum efficiency, it

---

[67] ER 30. http://www.dh.gov.uk/en/Managingyourorganisation/NHSFinancial Reforms/index.htm

[68] ER 27. http://www.phoenixfutures.org.uk/Filestore/Service_Literature/PF_ residentials_Generic_draft_-_final_v2.pdf

would have a throughput of 18 people, a 50% success rate would mean 9 people being drug free per year. Their income for 2010 was £342,773 [69] making the cost of successfully rehabilitating drug offenders almost £40,000 per person. That is given that they were in full occupancy and achieved the 50% success rate. If not, then the cost escalates.

As we saw, in Chapter 2 page 8, the average package of care for residential rehabilitation per person per year was estimated at roughly £20,000. From my example above the cost of £20,000 per person would represent the cost for each individual person in residential care, not those who were successfully rehabilitated.

The annual budget figure for The Haven pales into insignificance compared to the budget for Phoenix Futures who run a residential unit in Glasgow and as a registered charity in Scotland (SC039008) had an income of £22,885,292 [70]. However, after further investigation I found this to be their total UK income, for which they have six rehabilitation centres and provide various community services throughout the United Kingdom. There is no breakdown which shows how much it cost to run the Glasgow unit.

'Phoenix Futures is a leading provider of services for people with drug and alcohol problems. We offer services within community, prison and residential settings in England and Scotland.' [71]

In looking at residential units I will be looking at these two units in particular, The Haven in Kilmacolm, and Phoenix Futures in Glasgow. Both are committed to recovery and not just harm reduction. The first centre I will be looking at is The Haven, in Kilmacolm. The Haven is run by a Christian Charity on strong faith based lines.

Then I will look at Phoenix Futures in Glasgow which is run by a secular organisation. While their Glasgow unit focuses on recovery, the group as a whole offers harm reduction programs as well as residential units throughout the United Kingdom. Karen Briggs, Chief Executive of Phoenix Futures says

---

[69] ER 25. http://www.oscr.org.uk/CharityIndexDetails.aspx?id=SC034641
[70] ER 26. http://www.oscr.org.uk/CharityIndexDetails.aspx?id=SC039008
[71] ER 27. http://www.phoenixfutures.org.uk/Filestore/Service_Literature/PF_residentials_Generic_draft_-_final_v2.pdf

'My view is that our ambition for people we work with stems from our belief that everyone has the potential to end their dependency and rebuild their lives. Whilst we deliver abstinence based services, we don't believe this prevents us from delivering harm reduction services.'[72]

In 2005-06 the Government commissioned a review of residential drug detoxification and rehabilitation services in Scotland and came up with the following statistics: 'There are 352 beds available for drug treatment in Scotland, situated across 22 services. Thirty-one beds are dedicated for use by drug misusers only; most are for drugs and /or alcohol misusers. Almost one-third of the beds and services are located in Glasgow, and all but one of these is available only to Glasgow residents. Eleven of the 15 NHS Board areas have a residential facility and many are available to clients across the country.' [73]

These figures have shown a slight increase since then. In an answer to a written Parliamentary question on 19th January 2010, Fergus Ewing MSP, and Minister for Community Safety, said:

'The National Directory of Drug Treatment Services, maintained by the Scottish Drugs Forum, lists 27 residential services with 446 beds. This includes one residential drug crisis centre with 12 beds.' [74]

As we can see this is an increase of 94 beds (27%), which in this climate has to be commended, however I should point out that the 12 beds in the residential crisis centre, as seen in chapter 2, are part of the harm reduction program and do not represent residential recovery care. Also, although the beds may be available, the question that has to be asked is, are they being used?

'Occupancy rates varied from 36% - 96%. On average, services reported operating at around 80% occupancy, although several were at over

---

[72] ER 27. http://www.phoenix-futures.org.uk/Filestore/Service_Literature/PF _residentials_Generic_draft_-_final_v2.pdf

[73] ER 13. www.scotland.gov.uk/resource/doc/180429 *Review of Residential Drug Detoxification and Rehabilitation Services in Scotland.*

[74] ER 28. http://www.scottish.parliament.uk/business/pqa/wa-10/wa0119 .htm

90%. 100% occupancy is not attainable because of clients dropping out of treatment and the flexible nature of residential programmes.' [75]

Of the 22 residential facilities in the 2005-06 report, 8 provide only detoxification services, 7 provide both detoxification and rehabilitation services, and only 7 of them are dedicated to rehabilitation. The majority of these services treat clients with either, or both, drug and alcohol problems, only 2 are drug-only services. This reflects the common co-occurrence of drug and alcohol problems and is reflected in community based services. [76]

The number of beds per service ranges from 2 and 104. In general, the number of beds in any facility is fairly small: on average between 2 and 12. Castle Craig, with 104 beds, is the clear exception. Government statistics take into account the total number of beds, whether being used as part of a Government run programme or by private patients. While Castle Craig has 104 beds in 2006-07 only 21 people were referred there by Greater Glasgow & Clyde Alcohol & Drug Action Teams. Castle Craig was the only residential care centre to be named in the 2005-06 report, mainly due to its unusual size. They take private patients as well as NHS, interestingly I found it to be Christian based: 'Castle Craig continues to value the original Christian and spiritual heritage which shaped its work, recognising the uniqueness of each person and their right to pursue their own search for meaning and spirituality' [77]

Castle Craig uses the 12 step program and recognises a spiritual side to healing.

The duration of residential programmes varies, detoxification ranges from 1 to 12 weeks, with around 2 to 3 weeks being most common. Short-term rehabilitation lasts from 4 to 12 weeks and longer term programmes can run for anything from 3 months up to 18 months. On average, rehabilitation programmes in Scotland last around 6 months, with intermediate care at a halfway house recommended, this usually

[75] ER 13. www.scotland.gov.uk/resource/doc/180429 *Review of Residential Drug Detoxification and Rehabilitation Services in Scotland*
[76] ER 13. www.scotland.gov.uk/resource/doc/180429 *Review of Residential Drug Detoxification and Rehabilitation Services in Scotland*.
[77] ER 31. http://www.castlecraig.co.uk/about-us

lasts a further six months. In July 2006 there were 160 people on waiting lists for residential rehabilitation; given that there were only 352 beds at that time, this meant there was a waiting list for almost half of the available beds.

The 2005-06 survey showed that 63% of these patients will complete the course which would appear to be a high success rate. However 22% of the inpatients at any one time are readmissions, for a second or even third time; no figures are available for those who actually remain drug free. Alcohol and Drug Action Teams (ADATs) provide a wide range of support services for clients, from waiting to go into residential care to aftercare services, this also includes support for their families. There are, however, no follow on figures for people who actually remain drug or alcohol free for any proportionate length of time. Mark Easton's report [78] I referred to in Chapter 1 would seem to support that the figures for continuing abstinence are actually very low. The main problem in collating these figures is that once the addicts have completed the courses the follow up is voluntary. Many consider themselves cured and therefore find follow up programs intrusive and unnecessary.

As I showed in Chapter 1, no matter what form of rehabilitation or detoxification process the addict tries, whether it is in the community or in a residential setting, it is essential they have a good support network that they can trust. This is where being placed back into a new community after rehabilitation, such as a church fellowship, has an advantage as it immediately provides a new circle of friends and associates away from their old circle of friends who may still be using drugs. Many of the people on these programmes have had run-ins with authority and as we have seen can view them with a degree of suspicion; social services, housing associations, and police are all seen as threats instead of the support groups that they are.

Two approaches to inpatient care, Christian and secular

Firstly, I will look at what each service offers and how they operate then I will compare them.

---

[78] ER 1. http://www.bbc.co.uk/blogs/thereporters/markeaston/2008/10/drug_treatment_officials_were.html

The Christian inpatient service I looked at does not get direct funding from the Government, and Social Services do not refer people there due to the overtly Christian nature. They are, however, funded through Local Authorities being prepared to pay the housing benefit and support benefits due to the service users directly to The Haven to pay for the residential care and support offered. This covers approximately 50% of running costs, the rest coming from donations.

The Haven, Kilmacolm

Located in the countryside between Greenock and Kilmacolm in Scotland, The Haven offers accommodation and a community approach as a response to the problems of drug and/or alcohol abuse.

'The Haven Kilmacolm is a registered charity and has been in existence for over 18 years (formerly known as the "One Step Trust" and affiliated to Teen Challenge Strathclyde) working in the community providing significant support and accommodation to young men aged 17-40 involved in alcohol and drug misuse in order that they may become free from their addiction.' [79]

The Haven is a Christian organization working with the afore mentioned Teen Challenge, it has chosen to work with people labelled as vulnerable, disadvantaged, excluded and marginalized in order to give them the opportunity to have a very different future.

'We believe that every individual is of value and worth and that every individual has the capacity to change with the appropriate support.' [80]

The Haven is a 12 bed residential rehabilitation unit with a further 6 places available in a purpose built halfway house. They provide rehabilitation in an overtly Christian atmosphere. The addicts arriving at The Haven will be aware that they are coming to a place run by Christians and run on Christian principles, they are required to attend chapel every day and take part in Bible studies. The admissions criteria for the Haven make the Christian ethos of The Haven clear. People who do not have a personal faith are welcome on the understanding that participation in the Christian aspects of the community is mandatory. The rural location is ideal for breaking some of the networks which trap

[79] ER 23. www.thehavenkilmacolm.com
[80] ER 23. www.thehavenkilmacolm.com

so many people with drug and alcohol problems and gives them the opportunity to reflect and change enough to make it back into the community. The primary concern of The Haven is:

'To enable individuals who have, or have had, a drug and/or alcohol problem, to live a drug free, healthy and socially rewarding lifestyle in accordance with Christian principles' [81]

The service provides support, assistance, advice and counselling in a community setting. The centre's facilities include a small gym, games room, dining area, lounge area, all weather football pitch, and a garden with a pond and patio area.

The day starts with a time in the Chapel followed by Bible teaching and a discipleship program. This involves teaching on the basics of living the Christian life and having a personal relationship with Jesus Christ. There are work groups and chores to be completed, as they progress they will be introduced to work programs in the community and attend classes at the nearby college. The program is designed to provide a holistic approach to healing which includes the spiritual side. Their belief is that without a spiritual healing, the addict will never be completely healed. Their hope is that the Christian ethos delivered through the staff's faith is being expressed through love and is relationally driven rather than policy driven. The atmosphere pervaded by the staff is one that is not lost on the residents. While there I had lunch with the staff and residents, everybody eats together. I asked the residents, which for most of them was not their first attempt at rehabilitation, what was the main difference they found from The Haven to other rehabilitation centres they had tried? They overwhelmingly said, 'the lack of violence.'

The home is professionally run with 8 full time staff, 5 part-time staff and 6 regular volunteers. The staff and volunteers are all fully trained, and the support workers and management are trained in SVQ Care. Training is also offered in Health & Safety, First Aid, Stress Management, Pastoral Skills and Managing Difficult Behaviour. Staff

---

[81] ER 23. www.thehavenkilmacolm.com

are also encouraged to look at training required for personal development.[82]

'The benefits the program aims to provide are

- Build self-esteem and self-confidence
- Provide the opportunity to develop life and employability skills
- Increase social interaction
- Encourage and promote independence
- Promote problem solving and decision making skills
- Improve quality of life by promoting positive life choices
- Restore family relationships
- Help individuals to take responsibility for their own learning and their own lives
- Enhance social development and build relationships through shared experience
- Provide opportunities to get back into education and employment
- Support physical, emotional and spiritual development' [83]

Success at The Haven would be described as someone leaving drug free, having dealt with any issues, who will have a relationship with Jesus Christ, be plugged into a local church and either working or on a training program, a completely changed life.

A changed life

Tommy's Story – Tommy had been a heroin addict for eleven years, he had tried a private clinic, a drug rehab centre and the USA for help nine times, with no success. In March 2008 Tommy was invited to church where he heard about and experienced the unconditional love of Jesus Christ. Six weeks later he went to 'Broken Chains', a Christian outreach

---

[82] ER 23. www.thehavenkilmacolm.com
[83] ER 23. www.thehavenkilmacolm.com

program where he heard about The Haven drug rehab program. When I met Tommy he was completely drug free and, having completed 18 months at The Haven, was now a trainee support worker. Tommy says:

'I have so much going on in my exciting life and have to pinch myself sometimes. I have so many people to thank; so many people have made a positive impact in my life over the last 21 months – to each one I am very grateful. In the Bible, Jesus tells us he will be a solid foundation of rock for our lives:

"He is like a man building a house, who dug down deep and laid the foundation on rock. When a flood came, the torrent struck that house but could not shake it, because it was well built." *Luke 6v48*

Without Christ as my foundation I know I would crumble at the first sign of trouble.' [84]

Phoenix Futures, Glasgow

Located on the outskirts of Glasgow city centre, Phoenix Futures offers residential accommodation in what is called a 'Therapeutic Community' for drug and alcohol misusers.

'Phoenix Futures is a leading provider of services for people with drug and alcohol problems. We offer services within community, prison and residential settings in England and Scotland. Referrals are accepted from adults and couples aged 18+ regardless of gender, race, religion, sexuality, HIV status or disability.' [85]

Phoenix is a secular run charity which focuses on the marginalised of society in the drug and alcohol misusers, in order to give them a hope for the future.

'Every person who is dependent on drugs and alcohol has the potential to rebuild their life. This is our vision' [86]

---

[84] ER 29. http://www.thehavenkilmacolm.com/testimonies/tommys-story/
[85] ER 27. http://www.phoenix-futures.org.uk/Filestore/Service_Literature/PF _residentials_Generic_draft_-_final_v2.pdf
[86] ER 27. http://www.phoenix-futures.org.uk/Filestore/Service_Literature/PF _residentials_Generic_draft_-_final_v2.pdf

Phoenix house is a 39 bed residential rehabilitation unit; 12 of these beds are for women and are situated in a separate block. They also have a halfway house where people who successfully complete the rehabilitation programme can be assisted to return to the wider community. The service provides an abstinence-based (drug/alcohol free) residential rehabilitation and detoxification programme in a Therapeutic Community, so what is a Therapeutic Community?

'Our Therapeutic Community model for the treatment of drug abuse and addiction has existed for about 40 years. Therapeutic Communities are residential drug-free settings that use a hierarchical and stage based approach that provide increased levels of personal and social responsibility as clients move through treatment. Peer influence, mediated through a variety of group processes, is used to help individuals learn and accept social norms and develop more effective social skills.

On admission to the service you will be warmly welcomed by the whole community, including all staff. The Community is essentially the vehicle that brings about change - this model is called 'Community as Method'.' [87]

The service provides support and assistance in a safe structured environment. Visiting is limited to Saturday and Sunday afternoons and phone calls out are restricted. The programme consists of four stages, Induction, Primary, Secondary and Resettlement, how long an individual is in each stage will depend on the individual but in general it should take six months to reach the resettlement stage and then a further 6 months in resettlement. There are no quick fixes in rehabilitation.

Fully trained and professional staff offers a comprehensive therapeutic programme. Each individual is encouraged to look at the underlying reason for their dependency, this takes place in both sessions of one to one and in group sessions. As the resident progresses, they are encouraged to acquire new skills and develop a plan that will enable them to develop a healthy, drug free lifestyle and return to independent living in the community. Their day is fully structured, and

---

[87] ER 32. http://www.phoenixfutures.org.uk/Filestore/Service_Literature/ScottishResidentialClientGuide2010.pdf

they are involved in work groups in the general upkeep of the house and the grounds, gradually taking on more and more responsibilities. The residents have access to what is termed complimentary therapies, namely acupuncture and therapeutic massage.

The aim of the programme is to:

'Promote change by encouraging self-worth and personal responsibility, challenging individual attitudes and behaviour, and encouraging the development of life and social skills.' [88]

Success at Phoenix Futures would be described as someone leaving drug free, having dealt with any issues, and be able to cope with the outside world, living independently in the community. After leaving the service and remaining drug free for one year the service user is invited back for a graduation ceremony.

A changed life

'Gareth's Story - I joined the army at 18 and really enjoyed my chance to learn the bagpipes, but things started to go wrong when, after four years, I was discharged because I had begun to use heroin. I became seriously depressed and used all types of drugs to try and escape what was happening to me.

About a year later I met a man called Bruce Robertson from Progress2Work, Lothian and Borders. He had great faith in me and offered me support. With his help I applied for, and received, a grant from The Princes Trust for my pipes and set up my own business as a professional bagpipe player. Now I have a contract at Dalhousie Castle to play at weddings and more work is coming in all the time. With the help of Phoenix Futures, I've got myself from being a big time mess and serious drug misuser to getting off drugs, getting stable and setting up my own business. I feel really proud of that.' [89]

As we can see both facilities have the same goal, drug free changed lives, to offer hope and another chance at life. The main similarities are a structured daily routine, the acceptance of responsibility both for

---

[88] ER 32. http://www.phoenixfutures.org.uk/Filestore/Service_Literature/ScottishResidentialClientGuide2010.pdf

[89] ER 32. http://www.phoenixfutures.org.uk/Filestore/Service_Literature/ScottishResidentialClientGuide2010.pdf

their previous actions and life choices and accepting responsibility for what they are being asked to do. Installing a work ethic and time management ethic is important in both programmes, the residents' previous chaotic lifestyles have to be brought into order. Simple life skills have to be relearned, such as cooking and money management. Both centres recognise the need for continued support after the resident leaves their programmes. The better the support group the resident is released into, the better chance they have of continuing to remain drug free, the distancing from their previous drug culture is seen as important.

These are the similarities, what of the differences

The main difference is the focus on spirituality and the human spirit as part of the whole in The Haven while there is no direct spiritual aspect to the healing process at Phoenix Futures.

I also found that the Phoenix Futures programme was less relaxed. With visiting hours restricted to weekends, and phone calls allowed only at certain times of the day there is a definite feeling of being locked up. Obviously being in Glasgow this is only going to benefit the residents, but it takes a lot of the responsibility that they are trying to teach and instil away from the residents. The Haven benefits from being in the country, it is a long walk to any potential drug dealer, but the openness and feel to the place is very relaxed.

To compare the staff would be very unfair as both sets of staff are no doubt committed and sincere in their approach to their work. However, one report states that in general one of the key factors which help faith based organisations achieve success is because:

'They trusted those helpers more than they did staff at government agencies.' [90]

After years of perceived harassment by officialdom many who end up at Christian rehabilitation centres have:

---

[90] Sherman, Amy L., 2003. *Faith in Communities: A Solid Investment*. Society, January/February 2003. P.6.

'Dropped out of programmes run by different agencies that felt less friendly and more bureaucratic.' [91]

The fact that Phoenix Futures is also a charity and not just a Government run programme could possibly be helping it in achieving success.

Conclusion

The main problem I have had throughout my research is the lack of verifiable, consistent and comparable results. Government bodies want to justify their budgets, they are performance related and need results to show what they are doing is 'working'. Everybody wants to be successful, but what is success? The introduction of the 'harm reduction programme' can almost appear to be an admission that drug rehabilitation either does not work at all, is too expensive, or works so seldom that it is not worth trying. However, as we have seen, the statistics we are talking about are human lives. The tragic consequence of failing in drug rehabilitation can be death or a trail of shattered lives.

Harm reduction programmes are an attempt to alleviate the damage caused by drug misuse and therefore have to be valued for what they achieve. People living with controlled habits are on a start to something better. But we should never give up on the addict who wants to try rehabilitation 'one more time' just because it is expensive. We have heard from Karen Briggs, Chief Executive of Phoenix Futures who says:

'Our challenges now are to understand how we can cope with the cuts and whether we can convince those local communities that continued investment in drug and alcohol services is a good use of their limited money.' [92]

We should not have to fight for money to help people, The Haven constantly needs donations from well-meaning supporters to enable it to keep going and continue to provide the high level of service it does. The welfare of people should not come down to a budget. With the

---

[91] Sherman, Amy L., 2003. *Faith in Communities: A Solid Investment*. Society, January/February 2003. P.6.
[92] ER 27. http://www.phoenix-futures.org.uk/Filestore/Service_Literature/PF _residentials_Generic_draft_-_final_v2.pdf

continuing constraint on the Governments purse, faith based organisations are a way forward. In the Conservative and Liberal Democrats plan for the building of the 'Big Society', faith based organisations must be given a share of any funding without having to compromise their faith and beliefs. The giving of funding to communities must not exclude proven values which work, the commitment to fund the 'Big Society' has to be given to all. The Government says:

'We will support the creation and expansion of mutuals, co-operatives, charities and social enterprises, and support these groups to have much greater involvement in the running of public services.' [93]

From my research I have shown that faith based centres work. Perhaps because the people attending them appreciate that many of the staff are unpaid volunteers, and all the staff serve out of an unconditional love. At The Haven, the original facility was donated by a Christian family who still have an interest in seeing people's lives changed, and the money to support it comes from voluntary donations by Christians and not the Government. The residents see and feel that, it gives them an added incentive. That love expressed without expectation of anything in return may be the little extra incentive they need to keep going when they feel less able to. It may be that the spiritual awakening in them will bring them to a realisation that there is something bigger than themselves and that life does have a purpose to it.

'I know the plans I have for you, says the Lord, plans for your welfare and not for your harm, to give you a future with hope.' Jeremiah 29:11
As I have shown, the programmes that have a spiritual element to them (including the 12 step programmes) do have a better success rate. While people attending faith based programmes do not need to have a strong personal faith, I found that failure to engage with the faith principles of the regime will curtail their success rate on the programme. This would suggest that the personal faith of the addict is a major part of the healing process. Programmes with a spiritual or faith bases do work, they are worth supporting, but most of all, the people, the addicts, are worth another chance; who knows? they just might make it this time.

---

[93] ER 33. http://www.cabinetoffice.gov.uk/sites/default/files/resources/building-big-society_0.pdf

Danny Boy

Can the Ethiopian change his skin or the leopard its spots? Then may you also do good who are accustomed to do evil. Jeremiah 13:23

Much of our time and ministry has been to, let's say, some really interesting characters. We have been lead by God and His Holy Spirit to minister largely to men in their forties and fifties, sometimes younger. But men who have found themselves wrapped up in lifestyles that are leading them nowhere, and it has to be said in with many of them, they have accepted it and not only become wrapped up in their lifestyles but wrapped up in themselves. The key to deliverance from these situations is Jesus and the love and concern He will give us for others that takes our eyes of ourselves. That was the case with me, but taking that Good News and showing others the way out has become a daily challenge. Do they really want it? In our ministry we are led by the scripture:

When Jesus saw him lying there, and knew that he already had been in that condition a long time, He said to him, "Do you want to be made well?" John 5:6

We are constantly searching for those who want to get well. The answer Jesus got to the above question was not an immediate 'Yes' but an excuse as to why he was not well and how nobody helped him. Poor me. But we always have to be there in positions where we can offer the love of Christ and offering the help we are called to give.

We have met many 'loveable rogues' and some really nice young men who have just somewhere along the way lost it. Their solution to a problem, a very serious problem, has been to stick their head in the sand. The sand of drink or drugs or sex or gambling or so many vices out there, offering a quick fix for problems which years and years later still aren't fixed but indeed have got worse. Their heads are firmly stuck in the past with no hope other than death itself, which to many seems to offer the only relief. But we serve a God of hope and it is this message of hope that we take to a lost and dying world. We first got involved in this type of ministry when we were asked along to 'Broken Chains' by a couple we had met at New Life Church in Prestwick. It was held every Sunday afternoon in the church hall of the Episcopal Church in Fullerton Street, Ayr. It involved a time of worship, a testimony or something from the Word and a free meal. It was very popular, the ministry side of it was run largely by people from New Prestwick Baptist Church and from New Life Church Prestwick although others were involved. A rota of different churches took turns to prepare and serve the meals. It still continues today.

It was there that we met Danny, one of the first of many 'loveable rogues' and genuinely nice but lost people we were to meet over the coming years, many of whom have since died (we don't know Danny's current situation). We met Danny at Broken Chains one Sunday afternoon and immediately started to bond with him. He was an alcoholic and many a Sunday he turned up the worse for wear from the night before or perhaps after a quick swig on the way. He loved to worship particularly to 'Jesus on the Mainline' a Ry Cooder song which was a firm favourite at Broken Chains, the chorus always given gusto by all. He walked with a limp, had a stick and was due for a hip replacement but it wasn't happening as he often turned up for appointments full of the drink. When this happened he often had a short temper and ended up walking out or being put out.

We went to his house, we never realised people lived in conditions like that. (We have since seen that there are a vast amount of people living in such situations.) The ceiling was falling in, the doors were smashed and the kitchen and bathroom were disgusting. Danny sat and slept on a collapsed sofa and had a bucket in the corner for emergencies. His friend had his own chair which no one sat on because he was incontinent and sometimes couldn't even make the bucket.

The council wanted access to modernise the flat but were seldom able to get access, and when they did usually walked out. Danny had contact with other Christians, many of whom had tried to help him over the years, but he still continued in his drinking. We helped Danny as best as we could slowly, bit by bit. We spoke to the council and we agreed to support Danny while they got in to do the repairs. Meanwhile, we got him into hospital for his hip operation. While he was in the hospital the council came out to assess his property. He received a letter from them, they found his electric meter was rigged (dangerously so) and he was ordered to pay for a new meter and pay for the back electricity which they estimated was owed. It was pay up or be evicted. He had just received a large back payment for his benefits which we had helped him get from the social, so he agreed to pay.

He was still coming to Broken Chains and occasionally he went to New Life Church when someone picked him up. One evening we were coming to pick Danny up for a church service but when driving into his road a police van was coming out and Danny gave us a wave from the back of it with his stick. He was due in court the next day for non-payment of fines and the police came to put him in custody to make sure he would turn up. The police bought him a steak pie supper from the local chippy, he was just that type of a guy. We helped him budget to pay off his fines which were by now astronomical due to continuous non-payment.

When the time came round for Danny to have his house done, we supported him in a bed and breakfast which the council provided. But the first day the workman walked off the job. Jean and I had done a needle sweep but had missed one down the back of the wash hand basin in the bathroom. They charged Danny £50 for a needle sweep and the job continued. We supported Danny for a while, he now had his hip replacement and a modernised flat. He bought some new furniture but continued drinking. Jean supplied him with bottles of flavoured gassy water which she tried to encourage him to drink whenever he felt the need, instead of the gassy high alcohol cider he was drinking. He was always surrounded by drinkers and he didn't really want to 'get well', he just wanted someone to help keep him comfortable in his misery; the time came when we had to say 'enough is enough' and leave Danny to his own, (or somebody else's) devices. We learned a lot in our time with Danny and have no regrets or bad feelings about our time with him.

We are called to love the lost and he was certainly lost, does he remain lost? Only God knows, but seeds have been sown not just by us but by many faithful Christians and we believe God's word does not return to us void. Can a leopard change his spots?

"The wolf also shall dwell with the lamb, The leopard shall lie down with the young goat, The calf and the young lion and the fatling together; And a little child shall lead them. Isaiah 11:6

Only by the grace of God, which through Jesus Christ is made available to all who will receive him as Lord and Saviour.

and saying, "The time is fulfilled, and the kingdom of God [a] is at hand. Repent, and believe in the gospel." Mark 1:15

Camino de Santiago

Blessed is the Man Whose Strength Is in You, Whose Heart Is Set on Pilgrimage. Psalm 84:5

The story of the Camino de Santiago is probably a book in itself, and as this is a book of short stories I will try and condense it without losing the awesomeness of the journey, a pilgrimage, a walk with God. It was May and for some reason we had ended up at a Glasgow picture house watching a film called The Way. It starred Martin Sheene and was the story of how he found himself walking the Camino de Santiago, an ancient pilgrim route across the Northern part of Spain, if you haven't seen it I would highly recommend it.

'The Camino de Santiago known in English as the Way of Saint James among other names, is a network of pilgrims ways or pilgrimages leading to the shrine of the apostle Saint James the Great in the cathedral of Santiago de Compostela in Galicia in north-western Spain, where tradition has it that the remains of the saint are buried. Many follow its routes as a form of spiritual path or retreat for their spiritual growth.'

The film follows what is known as The French Way (Camino Francés). 'The French Way is the most popular of the routes of the Way of St. James (Spanish: Camino de Santiago), the ancient pilgrimage route to Santiago de Compostela in Galicia, Spain. It runs from Saint-Jean-Pied-de-Port on the French side of the Pyrenees to Roncesvalles on the Spanish side and then another 780km on to Santiago de Compostela through the major cities of Pamplona, Logroño, Burgos and León. A typical walk on the Camino Frances takes at least four weeks, allowing for one or two rest days on the way. Some travel the Camino on bicycle or on horseback.' We returned home amazed and inspired but obviously this was something we would never do, we were not walkers, had no hiking experience at all and disappearing for four weeks well how was that going to happen?

That June, 2011, I graduated from University with my MA in Theology and Religious Studies, after which we went to our daughter and son-in-law's house in Chester for a holiday, while they were in the Maldives. During the holiday Jean said to me 'I want to walk the Camino de Santiago.' Now when Jean sets her heart on something, unless God specifically says otherwise, then it is going to happen, how was this going to happen? Well, it did.

Delight yourself also in the Lord, And He shall give you the desires of your heart. Psalm 37:4

Jean certainly delights herself in the Lord, so with God on our side we set about getting ready. We went to an outdoor shop in Chester and bought all the gear, the boots, the walking sticks, the rucksacks, the socks, etc.. We also ordered the book 'A Pilgrim's Guide to the Camino De Santiago: St. Jean - Roncesvalles – Santiago' by John Brierley, a must for those considering the walk. He breaks it down into thirty-three daily stages, it was to take us thirty-five days, not bad for beginners. Thirty-five days of walking an average of 14 miles per day, some longer, some shorter, across all kinds of terrain, mountains, hills and plains and, at the time of year when we were going to be walking, it would be in hot temperatures, particularly for a couple used to the climate in Scotland, although we did live in France for a while.

We returned back to Scotland after our holiday in Chester and proceeded to give up our jobs and plan for the adventure. We drove up to the Carrick Hills, put our boots on, walked about 200 yards and said 'Yep, these will do'. And headed back home, duly prepared to walk 500 miles.

The first step was how would we get to St Jean Pied de Port in France? There was no easy solution to that, so we decided to drive there, almost 1200 hundred miles, crossing the English Channel en route. Well, when we lived in France we had regularly driven back to Scotland

and as we had a year old car, a Vauxhall Corsa, there was no problem in that.

We had no idea where we were going to leave the car while we spent five weeks walking the Camino but hey, details work themselves out, too much planning takes the sense of adventure and pilgrimage from it. My dad was concerned about this, ever the materialist, he said 'What about your car? You can't just leave it somewhere'. To which I said 'Dad, it's a lump of metal, besides if anything does happen to it, it's insured.'

We booked our first night's stay at 'Esprit du Chemin' an albergue in St Jean and from then on it would be by faith; every day we would arrive somewhere different and everyday depend on God's guidance to get us a bed for the night. We arrived in St Jean, left the car in a public car park near a small stadium and booked into our albergue: we were in bunk beds in a room containing another four sets of bunk beds. Quite a shock for a couple who had been married for the last 29 years and now found themselves in separate bunks in a room with eight other people. We registered at the Marie and received our 'Credencial' or Pilgrims Passport, we would have to have this stamped every day throughout our journey to prove we were genuine pilgrims in order to receive our Compostela 'The Compostela is a certificate of completion of the Camino de Santiago, and is issued to you by the Pilgrim's Office in Santiago de Compostela. There are two types of certificate: one is in Latin, and is issued to pilgrims who declare that they did the Camino for 'religious or spiritual purposes'. We then went back to our Albergue (Hostel) for a community meal where each person was invited to say who they were, where they were from and why they were doing the Camino. It was then into our bunks and a good night's sleep ready for the start of our journey. A good night's sleep was not to be had, with me one of the snoring culprits and Jean up at 5.00am getting ready for the off before anybody else was about.

We had a small breakfast and picked up a packed lunch that was prepared for every pilgrim leaving that day. We were off on the adventure of a lifetime but not before stopping at the chapel and lighting a candle and committing our pilgrimage in prayer to God. We were going to need His guidance and the strength and empowerment of the Holy Spirit, none more so than in the first few days ahead. The first stage from St Jean Pied de Port to Roncesvalles takes you over the Pyrenees. It is 15.6mile long and goes from a starting elevation of 550feet to a high point of 4,750 feet, straight up, and then straight back down steeply to 3,100 feet. By the time we were barely out of St Johns I had my first blister coming. But worse was to come. As we trudged on and on uphill a mist came down and round about the point in the film where the pilgrims son had walked of a cliff to his death, we were engulfed in mist. We sat down with our coverall black ponchos and got out the bocadillos our hosts at Espirit de Chemin had provided. There were no stops of any kind between St Jean and Roncesvalles, it was mountain country and no sign of civilisation anywhere. We saw some people turn back but we decided to carry on. Giving up on the first day wasn't an option, even if it was only temporary and probably common sense. My knees started to hurt, and my walking got slower and slower.

That was until I saw a sign for an Alburgue up ahead, we weren't expecting this, and I started racing a German guy (discreetly of course) to get any available room they might have, our wives were needing to stop, obviously. As I approached the 'Alburgue' I could see it was a concrete hut, no windows, no doors and a concrete slab for a bed. He could have it, very generous of me. My knees steadily got worse and worse and by the time we got to the summit I was in agony. Then as we started downhill into Roncesvalles I realised downhill was worse and more of a strain on my knees. I started walking backwards down the hill and when we eventually arrived at Roncesvalles we must have looked like a couple of wild things as we burst into the first small pension we came across, in our huge black ponchos, dripping wet, my face etched with pain and Jean's etched with concern about getting me somewhere to rest. She marched up to the bar and in her best French started to ask about a room, we however were by this time in Spain. Somewhere in the darkness and mist we had missed the border marker.

It was now getting late on in the day for new pilgrims to be arriving as it had taken us over eleven and a half hours to walk something which should have taken five or six with a break, would the rooms be taken? Would faith in God's guidance work? Yes, they had a room, it was upstairs, I hobbled up the stairs with Jean's help and crashed into bed, Jean sank into a hot bath. Never had we spent a day quite like this, we were thinking we must be mad, but something inside felt alive.

The next morning, we got up and headed for Larrasoana, 17miles away. Even without my sore knees we weren't going to make that, we got as far as Viskarret, seven and a half miles. We stopped at a small pension where we met Jo, a girl from Belgium, we were the only three pilgrims in the place, most others being able to go further on the first day in Spain. Jean enjoyed chatting to Jo and sharing her testimony while I sat and grimaced with pain. My knees had slowed us down quite a bit and that night as I lay in bed trying to get to sleep one of my knees seized up, I couldn't straighten my leg and the agony was tremendous, I had tears in my eyes. We had twin beds so I called over to Jean and asked her to come and lay hands on my knee and pray for my healing. Within five minutes the pain had gone, my leg stretched out and I fell asleep. During the night I got up to go to the toilet and as I put my hand on the room door Jean started to pray in tongues, I said 'Jean it's just me I am going to the toilet'. She was amazed that I was able to get up on my own. Praise God. She continued to do spiritual warfare until I returned from the bathroom and we both fell asleep.

The next day we set off again. By this time, my blisters were more than just blisters. The skin was coming off my heels. Jean in a Holy Spirit moment decided to wrap them up in toilet paper; as the day wore on and my feet sweated, the toilet paper moulded round my ankles and heels and gave me support. This was how my feet got the chance to heal. God's wisdom in man's torment. We only got as far as Zubiri which was still three miles short of Larrasoana. Pace was really slow, my knees still hurt and it was a steep downhill into Zubiri. As we crossed the bridge into Zubiri a woman asked us if we needed accommodation, we said yes as we had no idea where we were going to stay and didn't want to trail about any more than we had to. She took us to a private house where we were given a room with a double bed which we were allowed because we were married. The first thing we saw when we arrived was a picture of Jesus welcoming us. I went to a pharmacy and got some straps for my knees and the next day we continued on. By this time, I was thinking that maybe if I could just get to Pamplona I could get a train back and get the car, oh ye of little faith, I didn't want to do permanent damage to my knees and perhaps Jean could meet up with Jo and walk with her.

We kept walking in the strength of the Lord, people we passed were concerned about me and wanted me to get a taxi. We plodded on in the strength of the Lord through Larrasoana and headed towards Pamplona, not with any real intention of getting that far but just to see where we would get to. We came to a steep downhill and we both walked backwards down it; when I looked up we were in Arre, just 3 miles short of Pamplona. We stayed there at a Monastery, to get to our rooms we had to pass through the Chapel, it was such a place of peace and so restful. God was strengthening me, but I still needed that complete healing that would let me finish the Camino. The next day we passed through Pamplona and on towards Puenta La Reina. We had planned to stop at Zariquiegui but there were no rooms anywhere. Zariquiegui is just before a steep climb round the side of a wind-swept mountain and then a steep descent into Uterga where we stayed the night in a luxurious double room. Next day we got to Cirauqu. The woman who ran the Albergue was concerned about my knees and suggested anti-inflammatories, we prayed and went out into the sunshine. There was a small circular Chapel there with just one room and seats around the edges, none in the middle. The woman at the door kept kissing and cuddling Jean before leading her into the centre of the room where Jesus was and told her to sit in front of Jesus with her hands out to receive a blessing. That night at the Albergue we were allocated seats at the pilgrim meal where we were beside a German couple and an Italian couple, they had passed us with me struggling along the street, by this time I had grey stubble to go with my grey face, I was managing but I still had pain and still was believing for my complete healing.

The next day we walked 13 miles as far as Irache. All throughout the Camino there are fountains of water for Pilgrims to refresh themselves with. Here on the outskirts of Irache there were two fountains, one of water and one of red wine. I decided that I was going to take Communion and believe for my complete healing. I looked for something to put the wine into and I was just about to put my water bottle up to it when someone said 'that is not the spirit of it, you just take a little.' He gave me a small plastic cup and I took Communion and thanked God for my healing through the blood of His Son Jesus Christ. We walked into the first hotel we saw; it was like heaven, as we stood in an air-conditioned reception a woman came forward and gave us two chilled fresh orange juices. The room was first class with a bath, I went out and got myself some razors and the next morning, clean shaven and completely healed we headed off to Santiago, 410 miles away. By the grace of God, a miracle of His healing I made it, every step of the way. Praise God from whom all blessings flow. The next day we were in Torres marching down a steep street towards a pizza place when we met Jo from Belgium. She could not believe that we were still going and that I had completely recovered, but the evidence was in front of her, here I was striding down a hill (down being something I had really struggled with) and looking refreshed and marching on.

That was eight days into a thirty-five-day journey which will live with us for the rest of our lives. The miracles and the grace of God we saw throughout that journey as we travelled every day in His strength were something that money can't buy and people who have never experienced can never truly understand. But God is good, and God is faithful. He will give you the desires of your heart, you may have to go through a little pain and hardship but at the right time God will be there and while you are waiting just wait well and believe.

And He said to me, "My grace is sufficient for you, for My strength is made perfect in weakness." Therefore most gladly I will rather boast in my infirmities, that the power of Christ may rest upon me.
2 Corinthians 12:9

Homeless

And Jesus said to him, "Foxes have holes and birds of the air have nests, but the Son of Man has nowhere to lay His head." Matthew 8:20

In 2011 we were declared homeless, much to our surprise, but it's amazing how simply and quickly homelessness can become part of your life. In 2006 we gave up our home in Spilsby, Lincolnshire, and moved back to live with Jean's mum and dad to help out. We were originally coming for six months but had pretty much burned our bridges as far as going back to Lincolnshire was concerned, I had given up my job and we had given away all our furniture, we had decided to follow Jesus, no turning back, no turning back.

We had never lived in a council house in our 22 years of marriage. Up until we left France in 2000, we had owned our homes and from 2000 until now in 2006 we had rented from private landlords. But when we moved back to Scotland in January 2006, I felt it right to put our names on the council housing list. Jean agreed, neither of us knowing why, but God did.

We moved in with Jean's mum and dad, staying in the room Jean was born in, talk about going back to your roots. At first with both her dad, Jim, and her mum, Nan, then, after her dad passed away, with just her mum and finally just the two of us. Nan had developed dementia and it had become so bad that she had to go into a nursing home, much against Jean's will. One of the reasons we came back to Scotland was so that Jean's parents would not have to go into a nursing home. But it was taken out of our hands. The health service had advised us that before Nan becomes too ill, the family should hand over guardianship of Nan to them, the reasoning behind this was that families always leave it too late to make the big decisions and for the benefit of not just Nan but for Jean and her sister Janette that decision should be put into the hands of the professionals. This sounds great, but when the time came that Nan had to go into a home it meant we had no control over the situation and were obliged to agree. The situation behind Nan being eventually put into a home was quite distressing but correct and, to be honest, would only have been made more distressing if left to the family. In the end, hard though it was, it was a blessing to have the decision taken out of our hands. But it still wasn't easy.

While still living in Jean's mum and dads old house we went on a pilgrimage and when we returned from our pilgrimage at the end of the summer in 2011 we decided that it was no longer appropriate to be staying there. It was obvious by now that Jean's mum would never return home and we felt that our reason for being there was finished and that this season in our life had come to an end. We started praying and making plans for our next season. We started making plans to go to Chester and look for work. Our daughter and son-in-law lived there, and it would be good to be near them; being a more prosperous area we felt we would have no problem in picking up jobs there. Not knowing what area we would end up living in, and unable to commit to six months' rent we decided to buy a caravan and live the gypsy life while we looked for work. We sold our small Vauxhall Corsa and bought a Volvo S40 and a caravan.

Meanwhile, we got a letter from South Ayrshire Council wanting to update our housing application file, we had no more mind of even making the application we had never been offered a house in five and a half years. I phoned them and explained our plan, we had bought a caravan and were moving to Chester. The girl asked me what kind of caravan, I said 'A tourer.' She then informed me that a touring caravan was not a legal address and therefore we were homeless, did we want to make an appointment to come in and see her? We made an appointment and went to visit our local homeless department, still not quite sure why, as we had already made our plans. It transpired that having a break in our address with no traceability of where we were living would cause us problems when we were looking at enhanced CRB checks, or even when setting up a new home with energy companies etc... By the end of the meeting we had been offered a maisonette in Girvan. Girvan was 25 miles away; we arranged to go and see this maisonette (not quite knowing what a maisonette was) even though we were sure we wouldn't take it, but God had other plans.

We went to see the flat (turns out a maisonette is a two storey flat) it was in one of five blocks of flats in the 'homeless' area of Girvan. It turns out that this was not the most desirable part of Girvan, but that's another story. We had to make a quick decision on the flat, so we said yes and headed off to Chester. Our reasoning was that, well it was cheap rent and would be handy for when we travelled up to see our families. It wasn't too long before we realised that Chester wasn't working. We couldn't get jobs anywhere. We even signed up for potato picking but it never happened, the machine kept breaking down. Because our address was Girvan, we had to sign on at Girvan Job Centre, it should have been once a fortnight but, despite the fact they knew we were in Chester looking for work, they called us into the office every week. If you didn't turn up for the meeting, you didn't get your job seekers allowance, if you weren't on job seekers allowance you didn't get housing benefit. We had no option but to travel a 500 mile round trip, every week, in an old Volvo, that was costly, all our benefits went on petrol and we were living off our savings which were disappearing fast. At this point Jean said, we are in disobedience, God wants us in Girvan. We repented and made plans to go back to Girvan.

We put our caravan on ebay and waited for someone to make an offer. One day we had a knock at our caravan door. Somehow the owners of the caravan park had got to know we were selling our caravan on ebay. Unknown to us this, was not allowed. We took the caravan off ebay and started praying 'what now?' We did not want to take the caravan back to Scotland with us. For one thing there was nowhere we could park it at the flat. There was a man on our site who was a security guard and stayed in a DIY camper van on the site during the week. I said to Jean that man's going to buy our caravan. Jean said well go and see him. I went to him and asked him if he wanted to buy a caravan complete with a large awning for his guard dogs. He came over and saw the caravan and we agreed a price. He said if you want cash, I need to get to the bank but if you'll give me your bank details, I'll transfer the money in now.

I said we aren't planning to leave until Saturday (this was Tuesday) he said that's fine with me just leave it the way it is, I'll see the site owner and take over the site fees from Saturday.

That Saturday we left the caravan and awning behind in Chester and headed for Scotland. On our way up the motorway there were warning signs 'Caution, High Winds'. Thank you God for selling the caravan, so we weren't towing a caravan, we were in our solid low lying Volvo, driving smoothly home to where God wanted us.

This is LA

For we walk by faith, not by sight. 2 Corinthians 5:7

In 2011 Jean and I ended up living on the West Coast in LA. Unfortunately this wasn't the West Coast of America but the West Coast of Scotland, and it certainly wasn't Los Angeles it was Linden Avenue, five blocks of flats in the town of Girvan, Ayrshire. How we ended up there could only be God, we had no desire to live in Girvan and, if we had gone by reputation, we certainly would not have chosen Linden Avenue, but it turned out to be some of the best years in our walk with God.

We had been classed as homeless (see chapter 40) and were now living in Girvan, as I say, in Linden Avenue. After making the decision to take the flat and after God showing us that Girvan was where we were to be, and not Chester, as per our plan, we eventually moved in. When I say we moved in, literally, we and only we, moved in; we had no furniture and very little clothes. We had returned from the Camino Pilgrimage having lived for five weeks with only what we could carry in our small back packs and, having planned to live in a small touring caravan, we down sized our wardrobes. We would both get jobs and when we settled, we would just buy new clothes, wrong. We had now arrived at our new flat and were both unemployed, clothes would have to wait, we had no furniture and no white goods for our kitchen, no cooker, no fridge no washing machine, nothing. We moved in with a garden chair and a blow-up mattress for a bed, with a couple of sleeping bags from the caravan. The view over the Firth of Clyde was breath-taking, the flat itself left you speechless. With bright pink and purple walls and no carpets it was not the house of our dreams. But we were here, what next?

We were given a voucher for £200 from the homeless department, we could either spend it on white goods (wasn't going to go far) or carpets, we opted for carpets. Our thinking was nobody gives you carpets but people often help out with other items. We had the stair carpet laid by the carpet company and I laid the rest of them to save some money and for our £200 we had a fully carpeted house, praise God. The homeless office gave us a fridge freezer (second-hand) and a microwave. We needed some furniture and oh a cooker, well we had a microwave. Someone bought us a second-hand cooker from BRIC a local charity shop (we donated it back to that same charity shop when we left Girvan two years later). Our daughter Kerry gave us a metal framed bed and people we met from the local churches rallied round and we soon had a couple of couches (ex-Baptist Church offices) a dining table and chairs, two armchairs (which we only recently gave away) and a small kitchen table. The last item we needed was a washing machine. A saintly woman from one of the local churches gave us a cheque and we were able to purchase a brand new washing machine, the only new item in the whole flat. (Having had that washing machine for nearly 8 years we have just had it replaced free of charge by Hotpoint on a manufacturer's recall notice. God is good.)

As I said the décor was a bit loud. We bought a large tin of magnolia and painted the living room, the hall, the bathroom (including the tiles) and one of the bedrooms. We splashed out for our bedroom and painted it white, with a feature wall papered with a roll of paper we got in a charity shop for £1. I used some of the wallpaper to make a matching shade for a bedside lamp. The kitchen ended up bright yellow with a DIY mural beach scene. The house was now our home, and we were to spend two amazing and blessed years there.

Unemployed

Work and you will earn a living; if you sit around talking you will be poor. Proverbs 14:23 (GNT)

When we eventually arrived in Girvan, we were both unemployed and it was going to stay that way for six months. I was 52 and my only previous experience of being unemployed was during the summer in 2001 when I was in between years at Bible college. We were in Horsham, West Sussex and being unfamiliar with the process of looking for work I went to the local Job Centre expecting to get help and guidance on where I could get work. Instead, the woman started going through a whole application process for unemployment benefit. I said I wasn't looking for benefits, I was looking for a job. She continued looking at her computer and said that she didn't think I had paid enough National Insurance contributions over the past two years to qualify for benefits. I said what about the last twenty odd years I had been paying, she replied that didn't count. I said I wasn't there for benefits, I was looking for work. I got up and left the office, walked down the street into an employment agency, signed up and started work the next day and never went a day without work all summer. I worked as a delivery driver, a kitchen porter, a factory worker and an 'envelope' filler until it was time to go back to Bible college.

This time however, I was looking for long term employment. As I said I was 52, and we had moved to a town with high unemployment. There is no chance of a job in the town, right, wrong, God was in control, but it was going to take six months before I started earning any money. The opportunities were few and far between but prior to moving to Girvan I had been a support worker for adults with learning difficulties. This was something I had never done before and I only got into this line of work through Nigel, a Christian brother who heard I looked after my father-in-law and suggested I apply to the company he worked for.

I got a job with them as bank staff and although I got very few hours, the money helped while I went through University. But the other side of the job, which I didn't see coming, but God did, was that I had experience (however limited) and a reference to offer the one and only employer in Girvan willing to employ 52 year old workers, praise the Lord. Quarriers has an office in Girvan and Quarriers are a charity started in 1878 by a Christian business man; as part of their charitable work they now supply support services to adults with learning difficulties and in the months to come I would end up working with them. I have found out that the transition from being unemployed to being employed is not as smooth as you would expect.

Firstly, I was bank staff, so I had to work a month before claiming the wages I was due, only to be told that I would be paid at the end of the following month. Two months between starting and getting paid. The other thing was that now that I was working, I no longer qualified for housing benefit and I received a bill for £200 for overpayment of rent benefits. I further received a bill for £200 for overpayment of council tax benefits which they now wanted back. Despite the fact that I had kept them informed of my employment status, the housing benefit office had managed to overpay me and now wanted it back. I paid one of them from my first month's wages but had to pay the other over four months. It took a long time from signing off the unemployment benefit to actually being better off financially, but it was worth it.

God tells us it is good for man to work. We learned a lot of good budgeting skills (rather Jean learned a lot of good budgeting skills) during this time. It also gave us an insight into another world of unemployment, homelessness and the difficulty people can come up against even after they get a job. In fact, getting a job can add a lot of stress rather than taking away stress; that shouldn't be so, there should be more support for people, making that transition less daunting and easier financially. For people being offered low paying jobs the transition often seems to them more bother than it's worth, especially when they end up working 30/40 hours a week and don't seem to be that much better off. But pushing through is worth it and the sleep of the labourer is sweet.

The sleep of a labourer is sweet, whether they eat little or much,
Ecclesiastes 5:12 (NIV)

Ode to Girvan

On the same day Jesus went out of the house and sat by the sea.
Matthew 13

In 2011 God wanted to move us to Girvan, it was not our first choice. This poem sums up how I felt at first and how I felt when God got His way.

Our new home town is Girvan
Or is that Girvin, Girrrvin,
Gir Vin, Gurvin,
GIRVAN.

The first time we came here
We drove through it fast,
We'll take the wee flat
But it's no' going to last.

We're going to Chester you see,
A new life, for my wife and me.
Chester's nice, and bustling with life,
Milder weather, no trouble or strife.

We've family there,
A daughter and son (in-law)
It'll be grand, oor master plan,
But Girvan? Naw.

We've arrived now in Girvan,
My wife and me,
A coonsel flat,
Overlooking the sea.

Its cold, it's windy,
Giy windy at times,
But the sea is grand,
As it lands on the sand.

The harbour, the boats,
And awe things that floats,
The hills all around,
The beauty abounds.

Girvan, whit noo?
It needs new life.
We'll bring it, me and ma wife,
We'll give them Jesus, where we got new life.

GIRVAN, it's no' that bad!

Foodbanks

"Then the righteous will answer Him, saying, 'Lord, when did we see You hungry and feed You, or thirsty and give You drink?
Matthew 25:37

And the King will answer and say to them, 'Assuredly, I say to you, inasmuch as you did it to one of the least of these My brethren, you did it to Me.' Matthew 25:40

In 2012 after having lived in Girvan for a few months we came across a ministry at New Life church in Prestwick, that ministry was 'foodbanks'. This was a new concept for us, and we started praying about it. We also had a prayer meeting going on at the time in our house with a group of like-minded Christians from different denominations. As we were praying and meeting together, we started to have an open meeting in the Methodist Church in Girvan. No one from the Methodist church came, but Anne from the Episcopal Church, who met in the Methodist church building, and had use of the building, was part of our group along with Jean and I and others from the local churches. As we met, we had the doors open to welcome anyone who wanted to drop in. We had a meeting with Ellen who ran the foodbank from New Life and felt led by God to start one in Girvan. However, one day we had a visit from the local Methodist circuit minister who when she heard our plans said 'You can't just have anyone gathering in the church and inviting people in, I need to know what's your doctrine for this meeting, you will have to close it down and reapply in September to use our church'. My wife Jean said, 'I didn't know you needed a doctrine to feed the hungry and welcome the lonely and give them the Good News of Jesus Christ, I just thought that's what the church did'. We never did reapply, we ended up using the Church of Scotland's South Parish Church, and were made very welcome by the minister Rev Ian Mclachlan, despite none of us going to that church and incidentally none of us going to any Church of Scotland church. And the Methodist Church who closed our meeting down? Well, it's closed down now.

For the first three months of operating the foodbank at Girvan South Parish Church, no one came and when I say no one I mean no one. Jean, and her faithful band of volunteers, Yvonne, Becky, Anne and Margaret and myself when I wasn't working, turned up, opened up and waited and waited. At one point it was suggested that we should close the foodbank, but Jean said no, she was sure it was from God. The volunteers took the time to pray together and gel together as a team, ready for when the people would start to come, and they did. To this day, seven years later there is a foodbank in Girvan serving those in need in the community. Praise God.

When we moved to Liverpool in 2014 the first thing we did was start a foodbank. It has been a great ministry serving the local community and the occasional groups of asylum seekers. It has given us a great chance to minister to people who otherwise would not step inside a church. We believe the foodbank is not just a place where we can give out food to people who will go hungry again but a place where we can share the Good News of Jesus Christ, where we can offer hope to people in desperate situations, where we can offer prayer and where we can show the love that Jesus Christ has shown to us. As they share their stories of desperation, we can share our stories of hope.

But He answered and said, "It is written, 'Man shall not live by bread alone, but by every word that proceeds from the mouth of God.'"
Matthew 4:4

Once again, we have a great team of faithful volunteers. As we have grown together as servants of Christ we are now growing together as disciples of Christ. We have a meeting on a Sunday at 6pm at St Gabriel's where we gather together and study scripture and pray and support each other. This group includes those new to the faith and is open to all, we are looking to grow this group in the months ahead, reaching out to those for whom coming along to a Sunday morning service is just too much to expect. They can come along on a Sunday evening and be welcomed in a less threating atmosphere, especially for those who have been to the foodbank on a Tuesday and who will know most of the people who are there as they walk through the doors. We are believing God to see this group grow and grow not just in attendees but in discipleship of Christ.

The foodbank can be a hard ministry and often appears to be fruitless, but we believe that seeds sown will produce a harvest and that whether we see it or not is irrelevant; we are just called to be sowing the seeds of God's word, in season and out.

And let us not grow weary while doing good, for in due season we shall reap if we do not lose heart. Galatians 6:9

Milestone Christian Fellowship

Blessed Unity of the People of God. A Song of Ascents.

Behold, how good and how pleasant it is For brethren to dwell together in unity! Psalm 133:1

We have been involved in many different churches in our walk with God in the last 20 years but some stick out more than others, one of those was Milestone Christian Fellowship in Girvan.

When we arrived in Girvan, homeless and unemployed, we went to every meeting we could. Which involved The North Parish (C of S), South Parish (C of S) St John's (Episcopal Church), Girvan Methodist Church and Milestone Christian Fellowship (Baptist). Quite a mixture for such a small place and if you look at Girvan now one that reflects the battle God's people have everywhere while the Devil appears to be taking ground. The Episcopal Church building collapsed and after using the Methodist Church for a while has now closed down completely. The Methodist Church itself has recently been up for sale but still looks to be continuing, the two church of Scotland congregations have no Minister and are likely to have to merge, and the Baptist church building became unsustainable and they had to meet in the community centre, at least that was where they were meeting when we arrived. But God.

We enjoyed great fellowship with all the Christians we met in Girvan and were really blessed by their fellowship and practical help at a time when we had arrived somewhere we didn't know anybody and when materially we were struggling (i.e. we had nothing). We soon realised what it meant to be part of God's family. Milestone, the Baptist Church met, strangely, on a Tuesday evening and so that became a weekly place for us to go and somewhere we knew God was moving, despite the outward appearance to the world of a struggling church. Noel and Moya, were in charge of outreach and mission in the area and felt God had not finished with the Baptist witness in Girvan yet, and so it is proving. A new family from South Africa; Adam, his wife Michelle, and their two children Daniel and Charlotte had arrived in the area and there had been a connection with them. To cut a long story short, Adam ended up being the pastor there and they now have their own building again, (a former night club) and, despite some very difficult challenges, Milestone is to the fore again in taking ground for God's Kingdom.

We have many great memories of being part of this church and particularly enjoyed working with some precious Christians in starting the foodbank there. Also, the small beginnings of the Sunday morning service in the building site which was Adam and Michelle's home which were full of the Holy Spirit, taking Communion there was something special. When God moves you on it is hard when you have built up such special relationships, but He sustains you. While we continue to hold up in prayer all the Christians we met while living in Girvan, we especially think often of those at Milestone Christian Fellowship and the trials they have been through, the ones we know of and those we don't. It was a privilege to be part of them. While we don't go back or keep in touch, we are still with them in spirit.

But Jesus said to him, "No one, having put his hand to the plough, and looking back, is fit for the kingdom of God." Luke 9:62

Christmas Without Money, is Better Than Christmas Without Christ

For what profit is it to a man if he gains the whole world, and loses his own soul? Or what will a man give in exchange for his soul?
Matthew 16:26

I never really liked Christmas, for me it was a time of forced jollities, works night outs, you know be there or be square and who wants to be square, Christmas dinner with the family, buying cards for people you had hardly spoken to and wondering over gifts for people you wouldn't even buy a coffee for during the year. A good test for gift buying is if you don't know what the person would like or what they may already have, then you probably don't know them well enough to be buying them a gift. An excellent definition of Christmas for me was 'Buying people gifts they don't need with money you don't have, to impress people who couldn't care less.'

But then I discovered it wasn't about money. Well, that was a shock. One of the most wasteful Christmases I ever had was in France just before we became Christians. Sitting there drinking our glasses of champagne as we watched our daughter open parcel after parcel of things she hadn't asked for, didn't need and definitely wasn't impressed with. Then we found Jesus and the true meaning of Christmas or as we now define Christmas, 'Jesus, the reason for the season.' A bit naff but definitely true. But what about if there were no presents? No money? Would Christmas be the same? We were about to find out.

It was December 2012, we had run all our savings and resources out while running back and forward to Chester trying to make our plan into God's plan. Now I was in a job with no guaranteed hours. We had almost hit rock bottom while unemployed and waiting to get back into work. I had got a job as a Support Worker for adults with learning disabilities. I was bank staff and relied on the hours given out month by month. I was getting plenty of hours and we were doing ok. Then in October- November I started getting fewer hours. It wasn't until December I realised that the reason that I was getting fewer hours was because the contracted staff were nipping in and taking all the available hours as overtime for their Christmas pay. So when I got what would be my Christmas pay, there was nothing in it. We tithed, put in gas and electric (we had prepaid meters) and paid what we owed on other bills rent, council tax etc., put some petrol in the car to cover visiting Jean's mum in the nursing home (we walked everywhere else) and as we looked at what we had left we realised there was not enough to get us to our next pay, and we still had Christmas to get through. Jean had to phone her sister and explain to her that we would be unable to buy Christmas presents for the family this year as we had no money. Quite a far cry from when we were phoning them to come out to France for a holiday at our house with the swimming pool. By Christmas Eve we had £20 to see us through Christmas and we still had nothing for our Christmas Dinner.

We went to the local Asda to see what we could get. As we were walking along an aisle a woman staff member turns to Jean and handed her a joint of meat, she said could you use that I've just reduced it again. It was a joint of best silverside beef, reduced to £3. We bought that and some vegetables and had a delicious Christmas dinner. It was one of the most peaceful and Christ centred Christmases we have ever had and yes, Christmas without money is much better than Christmas without Christ. When you have Jesus, you have everything.

Then Jesus said to His disciples, "Assuredly, I say to you that it is hard for a rich man to enter the kingdom of heaven. Matthew 19:23

The opposite is also true, it is easy for a poor man to appreciate Christ when Christ is all you have.

God's Bank. £1,000. 2001 – 2012

Trust in the Lord with all your heart, And lean not on your own understanding; Proverbs 3:5

The last chapter ended with God providing miraculously for our Christmas dinner. That was the 25th of December (in case you didn't know) and we still had to get to our next pay day which was the 12th of January. Eighteen days away, with no money and no way of any money coming in, it was going to be a long bleak start to the year. But God.

We have always believed in tithing based on Malachi Chapter 3:

Do Not Rob God
"Will a man rob God? Yet you have robbed Me! But you say, 'In what way have we robbed You?' In tithes and offerings. 9 You are cursed with a curse, For you have robbed Me, Even this whole nation. 10 Bring all the tithes into the storehouse, That there may be food in My house, And try Me now in this," Says the Lord of hosts, "If I will not open for you the windows of heaven And pour out for you such blessing That there will not be room enough to receive it".
Malachi 3:8-10

And just in case you are saying that's Old Testament, then Jesus says,

"But woe to you Pharisees! For you tithe mint and rue and all manner of herbs, and pass by justice and the love of God. These you ought to have done, without leaving the others undone". Luke 11:42

But in the end whether you agree with tithing or not Jesus assures us that what you give away will come back to you.

"Give, and it will be given to you: good measure, pressed down, shaken together, and running over will be put into your bosom. For with the same measure that you use, it will be measured back to you."
Luke 6:38

It is strange whenever I write about money, I always end up putting more scriptures in than on any other subject. But what we do with our money shows where our heart is.

For where your treasure is, there your heart will be also.
Matthew 6:21

But you may notice that Malachi refers to 'tithes and offerings'. Tithes are easy in the sense that ten percent is ten percent, no question of that but what about offerings? How much should we give? How often? And to whom? Well, the simple answer to that is give as we see a need and as God leads us. In our Christian life we have given away two cars, a houseful of furniture, and various good quality white goods. We believe that if God asks you to give, you don't give rubbish. If it's not good enough for you it's not good enough for someone else. As for cash, we make gifts to various ministries from time to time, give money to help out others and we have never lacked. Jean got a scripture early on in our Christian life when we seemed to be giving away things that if we held onto, we would probably find useful later on.

For I do not mean that others should be eased and you burdened; but by an equality, that now at this time your abundance may supply their lack, that their abundance also may supply your lack—that there may be equality. As it is written, "He who gathered much had nothing left over, and he who gathered little had no lack."
2 Corinthians 8:13-15

So we felt free to give at times of abundance, knowing God would supply in the time of our lack.

In June 2001 we were still at Bible college and living off our savings when we felt called to make an offering to a large ministry of £1,000. We had never given a one-off gift as large as this but we prayed about it and believed God was saying to give it.

Now faith preachers, or prosperity Gospel preachers, will tell you that 'when a seed leaves your hand it goes into your future'. Our thousand pounds, which we would have spent in due course, was now in our future. Fast forward eleven years, it was the 28th December, we had no money, zero, zilch, however you want to put it, pay day was still fifteen days away. Then we got a phone call from a faithful brother in Christ who did not know our dire situation. He asked for our bank details, he had just returned from Goa where he had been selling his flat and wanted to bless us. He called back and said I have just put some money in your account. When we checked our account, it was £1,000, God had provided just in time. God may never be early, as we consider early, (where would the faith be in that), but He will never be late. The £1,000 we put into God's bank was there just at the right time, just when we needed it most, eleven and a half years later. God never forgets, He alone is faithful. Praise God!

Mia – The Biggest Why? You Will Never Answer

"For as the heavens are higher than the earth, So are My ways higher than your ways, And My thoughts than your thoughts". Isaiah 55:9

The above verse in no way explains the story I am about to tell and in no way suggests that God had a plan in what happened. Because the story does not reflect God's ways, but it does reflect the heart of love of God that can give us a hope. As I write this, my mother at 87 years old lies in an intensive care unit having being given a week to live four weeks ago; but still her body fights on and continues to keep her alive. I write this in the knowledge that the body has an amazing ability to survive against all odds; we are designed by God for life and survival. Yet that makes the story of Mia even more unexplainable.

One night while we were still living in Girvan, we received a phone call from Jean's sister Janette. Our niece, her daughter, who was expecting a baby any day had been to the hospital and was told that her baby was dead in her womb and that she would have to deliver it. What can you say to someone on the other end of the phone at times like these? We of course prayed for all the family and then we drove up to be with Jean's sister and brother-in-law, the expectant grandparents. Lynn and Stephen had their baby, stillborn, and named her Mia. They were then given a private room where they had the baby with them dressed and looking 100% perfect, yet with no life in her tiny body. We went to visit them, it was heart breaking and there are just no words that can comfort parents at times like these, certainly nothing that is going to answer the why. After a week they had to prepare for the funeral. To see that young man Stephen carry a small white coffin of a child they never even got to hear cry was heart wrenching, and to see all the family and friends gather round to support them and comfort them makes you realise how precious life is. We should never take this gift of life for granted and when life is taken away so unexplainably, we should never torment ourselves with the why? That question, it cannot be answered this side of heaven.

Just over a year later they were blessed with a son, Kai. It was a brave decision to try again so quickly and while I am sure they will never say Kai replaces Mia, they have a young son who they can, and do, pour their love into.

and the peace of God, which surpasses all understanding, will guard your hearts and minds through Christ Jesus. Philippians 4:7

Full Time (paid) Ministry

Stay there, eating and drinking whatever they give you, for the worker deserves his wages. Do not move around from house to house.
Luke 10:7 (NIV)

In March 2014 we came to Liverpool for a job interview for the post of Evangelist / Community Outreach Worker. Two weeks later we had given up everything in Girvan and travelled the 240 miles to start full-time paid ministry.

Ever since we first gave up our life in Toulouse, France, to go to Bible college in Horsham West Sussex we dedicated our whole lives to serving God; to be released into being paid for this and being able to do it without the distraction of earning a living elsewhere was a dream. We had prayed about it and left it in God's hands and almost fourteen years later it happened. Several times we had gone for interviews and, just prior to this post, we had been invited back for a second interview but turned it down as we didn't feel God was calling us there, it didn't feel right. It was a big step to turn down that chance, which may never have materialised but we just knew deep in our spirits that it wasn't for us and shortly after we got a call to come to Liverpool for an interview.

We met with the minister, after having arrived late due to getting lost just a couple of hundred yards from the Vicarage, and we were greeted at the door by a confident outgoing young woman who seemed quite at home answering the door, it was one of the other candidates. Later that evening I went for an interview with one of the wardens and another man from another church. I went back to the hotel and told Jean it didn't go well. We thought the young woman would get it. A short while later we got a phone call from David, the vicar, they wanted to offer us the job. The next day we went round to see David before setting back of home to Girvan, praising God.

After fourteen years we had begun to think paid ministry was never going to happen and we would have accepted that, but God had come through just at the right time. Neither of us had had any full-time work in that fourteen years but we worked wherever and whenever we could (tent making) and God was faithful. He always provided and we were blessed so often in that time. When you are continually living by faith and trusting in God it is challenging (especially after being used to a large wage) but also exciting, you see His hand in so many ways, many of those stories are elsewhere in this book. So, when after fourteen years you have a steady income and a house it can be a bit of a shock. You are never going to be rich in this type of work but, unless you fail to budget (Jean's department) you are never going to have nothing and therefore have to rely on God's miraculous provision in quite the same way; He has already provided. However, it has to be said we live beyond what you would expect someone on our income to be living on and that has been the grace of God.

When I applied for the job I said 'buy one get one free' Jean doesn't receive a wage or any benefits or any income of any kind and that is the way we have worked for over five years now. I am paid and Jean is the 'freebie', although it often appears the other way around. Jean is always very much in the thick of everything I do. It would be fair to say that without Jean my ministry wouldn't happen, her encouragement, support and Godly wisdom have kept me on track many a time and she could get a job anytime as a PA. The main challenge we found in ministry is often you think 'Am I doing enough?', 'Where is the fruit?'. Time management is hard and what do you count as time? Apart from the visible hands-on work, there is prayer time, preparation time, visiting time, pastoral time, listening time, just being out in the community time, being available time and keeping your lifestyle a vibrant and effective witness. But most of these things we have been doing all our Christian life, so what makes us 'payable', what makes us 'deserving of a wage'. Well only God can answer that one, we can only thank God for the blessing and make sure we are guided by His Holy Spirit and being obedient to Him.

Full time ministry is very demanding but being part of so many people's lives, sharing the Gospel and offering the hope that is Jesus Christ is an awesome privilege and responsibility and one which we take really seriously, and to God be the glory.

The Outworking of Love

By this we know love, because He laid down His life for us. And we also ought to lay down our lives for the brethren. 1 John 3:16

This is L8

"The Spirit of the LORD is upon Me, Because He has anointed Me To preach the gospel to the poor; He has sent Me to heal the broken hearted, To proclaim liberty to the captives And recovery of sight to the blind, To set at liberty those who are oppressed". Luke 4:18

From living in LA (Linden Avenue) we moved to L8.

L8 is an area of Liverpool which covers Toxteth, if you google Toxteth you will see it is infamous for the riots. These riots happened in the 80's, but more than thirty years later it still struggles to shake off this image. This wasn't helped when in 2011 the area was once again seen on television as home of a riot.

We were in Northern Spain walking the Camino de Santiago when we saw it on television, in the middle of nowhere on a screen in a café it caught our attention, for no other reason than the news was coming from the UK. We had no idea of Toxteth's history of riots and we certainly had no idea that three years later we would be living there. Further rioting broke out in Toxteth on the evening of 8 August 2011 - almost exactly thirty years after the most infamous riot - at a time when riots flared across England. Vehicles and wheelie bins were set alight in the district, as well as in nearby Dingle and Wavertree, and a number of shops were looted too. Two police officers suffered minor injuries as a result of the rioting. It was brought under control in the early hours of the following morning. Individuals arrested and charged in relation to the 2011 rioting were from addresses all across the city, with Toxteth residents being a clear minority.

The postcode L8, as I was to find out, is not a desirable postcode, especially when it comes to insurance. Having moved from a 'not so desirable address' in Scotland I was shocked at how much more a 'not so desirable address' in Liverpool was going to cost me. In fact, I gave up trying to insure my preferred mode of transport, a Volvo, which was going to cost us three times more than if we were to insure it in Scotland, and for fifteen months we had no car. When we eventually got a car, it was a Nissan Note small, new and much more insurable, but still more than twice what it would have cost me in Scotland.

Now for those of you reading this who come from either LA (Linden Avenue) or L8 (Toxteth), we have been greatly blessed while living in both these areas, but it has to be said that for two country cousins coming to live in a city for the first time, L8 was a shock. Police raids, an abandoned stolen car, a car chase ending in our close with Police cars in a scene like something out of a movie and a house having all their windows put in, it was a shock, and that was just in our street. Within close proximity we had stabbings, shootings, cars being set on fire, and gangs of youths roaming the street. Where would Jesus be, that's right L8.

Four years later we are still here, our street is quieter, and there have been none of the above types of incidents for over two years. Prayer and God's presence, brought about by the prayer and praise of God's people, makes a difference. There are still incidents near us, only last week a young man was chased into a carpark 500 meters from our home and brutally stabbed. We must keep on praying for areas all over the UK, and indeed the world, where violence is part of life. It has to be said that most, if not all, of the violence in our area revolves around drugs and the criminal elements that seek to ensnare and control people for their profit. The threat of prison is not a deterrent, it is seen as part of the lifestyle.

The only thing that will change this is Jesus Christ. We must be prepared to go where God calls us, knowing He is with us by the power of His Holy Spirit.

Greet Rufus - Chosen of The Lord

Greet Rufus, chosen in the Lord…. Romans 16:13

When we first arrived in Liverpool, we were just in time to be around for Kerry and Andrew when she had her third miscarriage, they were devastated and didn't know if they could keep on trying or not. That same week we were invited to a prayer meeting at St Philemon's who, along with St Cleopas church and ourselves at St Gabriel's, were part of the Toxteth Team ministry. They have a regular prayer meeting on a Thursday Evening called Prayer Central and to welcome us to Liverpool we were invited along. Brian asked us to come up and share a few words and asked for any prayer requests for our forth coming ministry here in Toxteth, which we gave him.

He then asked Jean if there was anything in particular personally that they might be praying for and Jean shared that our daughter Kerry had just had her third miscarriage and she and her husband Andrew were considering whether to keep trying or not. This was committed to prayer. We sat at a table with Lizzie who spoke to Jean and promised to keep Kerry in prayer. A few months later Kerry was pregnant, and much prayer was put into the pregnancy and the safety of the baby and Kerry.

In March 2015, almost exactly a year after that prayer meeting, we got a call, 'You have a grandson - Rufus Joseph Kettle' Joseph was Andrews middle name and Kettle their surname but Rufus? Never heard of anyone called by that name before, but hey what's in a name, we had a healthy baby grandson, praise God. That night when we got home, we were looking through our Bibles and came across Romans 16 v 13, 'Greet Rufus, chosen of the Lord'. Rufus, what a great name and what a great grandson, and to God be the glory, an amazing answer to prayer.

The effective, fervent prayer of a righteous man avails much.
James 5:16

52

God's Provision – Needing £3,000

And my God shall supply all your need according to His riches in glory by Christ Jesus. Philippians 4:19

When we arrived in Liverpool, we had no car. Previously in Girvan we had sold our car, a Volvo S40, and were using a van which had been purchased for us to help with the ministry we were doing in Girvan, the foodbank and helping people with second hand furniture. So, when we left Girvan, we felt it right to leave the van there. Living in a city was new to us and the availability of public transport and at a reasonable cost was a bonus, so we didn't have to jump in and buy a car straightaway until we were settled. Now by this time I was 54 and had owned cars since I was 17, so it was quite a shock. However, Jean, who had never, and still has never, had a licence, set about using the public transport. One day she decided to visit our daughter in Chester about 30 miles away. She walked down to the bottom of our street and got on a train at Brunswick station and within 40 minutes was in Chester visiting our daughter and the bonus, it was only £4.95 a return. We were car-less for fifteen months but then we decided it was time to get mobile again. We found a large part of our day was being taken up travelling, and during the winter it wasn't great.

At the top of our road someone was selling a Volvo S40, lovely looking car and cheap. I looked into the cost of insurance, not cheap. It was coming in at three and four times what I had been paying in Girvan. Turns out that living in a city, and particularly having a postcode starting L8, has its disadvantages. I estimated that the minimum I needed just to put an old Volvo on the road was £3,000, which incidentally we didn't have. Then a letter came through the post out of the blue saying that if you were over fifty-five you may be able to take any works pensions out early. I was now over fifty five and thought I would look into it. I had left British Aerospace in 2000, fifteen years ago, but I was sure I had a pension. So we prayed about it and looked into it. We ended up not going with this pension company, to be fair they ended up advising us to take what BAe were offering; although they could release a larger lump sum to us if that's what we wanted they couldn't match the pension and benefits of my works scheme. I had paid in about £13,000 over the years I was with British aerospace so I felt we could easily get the £3,000 we needed. But God. The lump sum I ended up taking was well above that and the pension that came with it has helped us be in full time ministry together without having to be scrimping or scraping and we are currently living a blessed life beyond what we dreamed of.

As for a car? Jean suggested we look at car leasing and after using some of the money from our lump sum as a deposit to bring our monthly payments down we took possession of a brand-new Nissan Note, with much cheaper insurance and ideal for city living, and all because we asked and believed God and let Him provide.

And my God shall supply all your need according to His riches in glory by Christ Jesus. Philippians 4:19

Turkey – The Country Not the Bird

*Now to Him who is able to do exceedingly abundantly above all that
we ask or think, according to the power that works in us,*
Ephesians 3:20

Now when God supplies, He supplies. When we were praying and asking and believing for £3,000 for a car, we would have been more than happy with £3,000 for a car but as it turns out God had more in store for us. He richly blessed us, so much so than when we needed a break, we had more than enough left over from getting a car. As I said in the last chapter when the money came, after tithing, we decided to go for a lease car, we paid a large deposit to keep the monthly payments down and we paid the yearly premium for our insurance, to avoid any monthly payments, we bought two funeral plans, helped our daughter and son-in-law with the deposit on their first home, cleared an old debt, blessed each other and put some money in the bank. As you can see, God is able to do exceedingly abundantly above all that we ask or think.

We had just started our two-week annual holiday and jumped in our new car and headed over to Chester to Andrew and Kerry's to see them and our four month old grandson Rufus. They were living in a rented two-bedroom terraced house in Hoole, Chester. On the way back, the weather was miserable and Jean and I looked at each other and said 'Is this our two weeks summer holiday?'

We went into Liverpool city centre, into the first travel agent we saw and asked if they had any late deals? Somewhere warm. As we sat with the girl, she gave us various options none of which were very great, then she said, 'Would you consider Turkey?' We said yes not really thinking much about it. It sounded nice, warm sunny days, temperature in the 30's. We would have to leave from London Gatwick early the next morning. We said we would manage that (about a four-and-a-half-hour drive, the new car was going to earn its keep.) She said you would need a visa, but she could do it online there and then if we had our passports. The price was unbelievably cheap and we decided to go for it.

I went home to get our passports, fortunately we live only ten minutes from the City Centre, while Jean went to Primark, a couple of hundred yards away, and stocked up with some summer clothes. We met up again in the travel agent and managed to conclude the deal at 5.30pm just as the shop was closing. We went back home packed a case and headed for Gatwick straightaway. We had decided to drive down that night and booked a hotel near the airport with car parking and a shuttle bus to the airport. It's nice to have the money in the bank to just do things like that on the spur of the moment, Praise God.

As we lay in bed at the airport hotel, we were looking at Turkey on the internet and there was the latest news. An ISIS terrorist had posted a selfie of himself on a Turkish tourist beach, complete with machine gun. No wonder the girl asked if we would go to Turkey. But our faith was in God, we believed He had provided for us to be going there and therefore we believed He would protect us.

We had a great holiday. Lying on a beach is not really our style of holiday, but as we lay at the side of the sea every day, dipping in and out for a swim, it was totally relaxing. The restaurants were plentiful and we had a nice hotel, the whole place was spotless, and the five o'clock prayers every morning? Well Jean just prayed in tongues against them.

When we came back from holiday Kerry and Andrew shared with us that they were looking at buying a house with a garden. They were saving up for a deposit and could we afford to lend them some money so that they could get a deposit together and start looking for a new home. They could afford the mortgage and it would actually work out cheaper than their current rent. We told them that when it came to the deposit whatever they were short of we would pay, and they wouldn't need to pay it back. Within a few months they had a three bedroomed semi-detached house with front and back gardens, and it was cheaper per month than renting. Praise God from whom all blessings flow. When God blesses you (abundantly) He blesses what is yours as well.

"Blessed shall be the fruit of your body... Deuteronomy 28:4

Camino de Finisterre - The End of the World

The LORD shall preserve your going out and your coming in From this time forth, and even forevermore. Psalm 121:8

After walking the nearly 500 miles of 'The Camino De Santiago' back in 2011, Jean and I had headed home from Santiago exhausted but elated. It had been the most exhilarating experience in our lives, walking every day for 5 weeks we were on a spiritual high. In the film which inspired us to walk our Camino, 'The Way' with Martin Sheene', the character he played had went on from Santiago to Finisterre which means 'The End of the World', another 60 miles from Santiago to Spain's North- western Atlantic Coast. We had decided then that enough was enough, and we would leave that for another day. Four years later in September 2015 we eventually made our way back to Santiago to walk the 60 miles to Finisterre. This is the story of our 'Camino Finisterre'.

After years of waiting for the right time (and the right price) we had our tickets to fly from London Stansted to Santiago de Compestela, we were on our way, same boots, same ponchos, same walking sticks, two small back packs for our week's 'holiday'. We had kept our luggage to a minimum so we didn't have to pay for 'hold baggage.' Jean still had her old walking sticks from our first Camino which were collapsible and almost fitted in her backpack. She was summoned at security and after having to empty her complete backpack, her sticks were confiscated.

When we arrived in Santiago to do our pilgrimage, we had no idea how we were going to get from the airport to Santiago or where we would stay that night. The idea of a pilgrimage is not to book, but to have faith. We ended up sharing a taxi with a couple who were heading to their second home in northern Spain, they were British but the man spoke Spanish and spent the whole journey arguing with the taxi driver who had started ranting and raving when he realised we wanted off in the city centre and the other couple wanted off at the train station. I have never seen a taxi driver turn down business quite so forcefully. They argued back and forth about how out of the way the station would be for the taxi driver, and despite our travelling companion seemingly holding his own in the argument, we all got off at the city centre. We went into the Cathedral to say a prayer for our Camino and then headed off to find some accommodation for the night.

We decided to start along on our Pilgrim route and look for accommodation on the way, but Santiago is a very small city and we quickly found ourselves on the outskirts heading off on the trail. We decided against this as it was getting late and we had been travelling all day, so we headed back into Santiago with no sign of any accommodation. Jean spotted a small bar and suggested we ask there if they had anything. The bar had no rooms but the guy who ran it started phoning around for us and after being unable to get us a room he said his friend had a cancelation, but it was for a whole house, did we want it? It was 70 Euros (about £45) for a whole house. While being dearer than what we wanted to pay (accommodation is cheap on the Camino) it was getting late, and we were running out of options. Turns out the house was just around the corner from the bar, it was spread over three stories and slept seven, it was lovely, a real gift from God.

To make up for the 'expensive' room we decided to get some food from the shop we had seen on the corner of the next street. It was literally a downstairs room in someone's house, with a limited supply of basic but fresh food. We stocked up with cheese, cold meats, fresh fruit and half a loaf (it was the only bread they had left, and I am sure it was the owners supper). We went back to our house and had a gourmet meal for our first night. Tomorrow we would start walking. We started off early in the morning keen to get back on the Camino; after a four-year break, it was great, what a feeling. Nothing but Jean, me and God.

The first stage of our 60 miles was from Santiago to Negreira, a distance of 14 miles. When you haven't done any kind of serious walking for four years it's a hard start, the terrain is uneven and the route goes to a height of 900ft. By the time we had arrived at Negreira, we knew we were back on the Camino. The restaurants weren't opening till 8'oclock, so it was into a supermarket for bread, cold meat, cheese and fruit. We certainly weren't going to put on weight. We ate and decided on an early night. Jean had struggled with the hilly parts of the walk and as she had had her walking sticks confiscated at Stansted airport, I nipped out to a small Chinese bazar I had seen and got a new pair of sticks for her. She was so exhausted she never even knew I had left the room but was delighted when she awoke to see a shiny new pair of walking sticks. (At the end of our Camino we left them at the side of the route prior to going to the airport so we wouldn't get them confiscated again. Jean got stopped by security anyway and no, Jean doesn't look like a terrorist).

Day two saw us start a 21 mile section, by the time we got to Maronas at about 13 miles we were ready to call it a day. As I said, the journey is by faith so we had no accommodation booked and a lot of people had decided Maronas was far enough, there was no accommodation available. We had no alternative but to keep walking, there was another Albergue (Hostel) outside Maronas which we decided to try, but again no vacancies, we walked on and got to a crossroads where our only option was to carry on. Our guidebook was showing no more accommodation for another 5 or 6 miles and the route was over a hill, it didn't look like we could make it before dark. Time to pray.

Our guidebook was showing a nearby hotel that would send a car to pick you up and then in the morning return you to the route in order to carry on. The problem was we had no Spanish and we couldn't get the mobile phone to connect with the hotel anyway. We spotted a small bar further down the road just off our route. Jean decided that it would be best if I hung back as I was already looking a bit wild (I had long hair which even after just a couple of days was looking unkempt and I was unshaven for about 10 days) Jean reckoned that was why we didn't get into the last place. The bar had only four men in it drinking coffee or some small drink, and we could see an old Spanish lady stirring a large pot in the back kitchen. I retreated and left Jean to get on with it, she came outside shortly afterwards and declared that a car would be there in five minutes to take us to the hotel, adding 'at least I think that's what I've arranged'. We watched each approaching car intently and then, sure enough, a car arrived with the driver shouting 'hotel'. We were off, God had provided. After a good night's sleep, we were dropped off early next morning back on our Camino.

We headed off to make up the time lost by our shortened walk, but it didn't take us long to realise we were going to have to split our journey over four days and not the three shown in our guide. We came to a thirteen kilometre stretch of high moors and headed for Cee; we reckoned if we made Cee today that would leave us a good size walk for our last day. Having walked for thirty-five straight days for the Camino de Santiago, to be talking about our last day already seemed strange. Although tired and stretched by walking 50 miles already, doing such a short Camino was going to be strange.

We arrived in Cee on a Sunday afternoon and were having difficulty finding accommodation, a large hotel on the corner was closed, although it was very definitely still in business which we confirmed a few days later when we were on our way back. You have to time your arrival carefully or be prepared for Spanish opening times. We eventually found a hotel which was open, more expensive than we wanted to pay but it was a short Camino so we could afford to splash out a little and, praise God! it was worth it with a large luxurious bath for the aches and pains. Jean had struggled a little today and had a sore back, wondering whether to take the last two pain killers or just have faith she decided on faith and a hot bath.

We were hungry, but not too hungry as we had eaten at lunchtime which was just as well as we had arrived too early for the evening meal. We went to the bar and ordered two cokes and the girl there gave us a plate with two free tapas, a welcome snack, which we took to our room, we enjoyed it so much that we decided on another coke and ended up with three more free tapas, which was ample for our evening sustenance, God provides when the hotels are dear. (60 Euros or 40 pounds, for a nice double room with a bath, as I say it is not expensive compared to the UK but relatively expensive when on a pilgrimage.)

The breakfast in the morning was great and set us up for the day, all you can eat, cold meat, cheese, toast, pastries, bread, cereal, yoghurt and fresh fruit. We were now all set to head for the 'End of the World'.

We walked through some beautiful countryside before heading down to the coastline for the last 2kms on a beautiful sandy beach. Boots off and bare feet, we headed for Finisterre. On arriving there we once again set about looking for some vacant accommodation. We headed down a narrow street in the direction of the harbour and while passing an Albergue a woman invited us in. We didn't want to stay in an Albergue but she insisted she had a room we could see. It was a typical Albergue, and as we entered it, we saw the reception desk, seating area for eating and the shared kitchen with someone preparing food, all open plan and all free for all to use. She took us through the back and up a staircase, the room she showed us was basic and it had a shared bathroom, we weren't impressed, she could tell. She then said she had one more room, she took us up to the third floor where there was only one room, which was bright and modern with a private en-suite bathroom, and to top it all we had a rooftop balcony as big as the room overlooking the town and the harbour and out over the sea. Perfect, we thanked God and prepared for the last part of the Camino.

We now had to walk to the lighthouse where this last stage officially ends. It was another 10k round trip, by foot, but was worth it. Here there is a fire pit where you can burn any excess baggage or footwear you no longer require, there is also a 'Peace Pole', but most importantly there is a Cross, where you can consider how little your suffering was compared to that of Jesus Christ when He went to his death on the Cross at Calvary. Praise God for His resurrection and our resurrection into new life now and into eternal life with God when we die.

That night in our rooftop room Jean saw something on the wall of our room, it was three crosses; there was no explanation of how these crosses, which looked like shadows, were on the wall but Jean got that 'to live is Christ, and to die is gain'. When we die to self, we truly live and, even should we die we will gain so much more for eternity.

For to me, to live is Christ, and to die is gain. Philippians 1:21

Next day it was back to Santiago, by bus. We headed for the Cathedral to give thanks to God and to take communion at the Pilgrims Mass. Then we flew back to the UK. It was too short but well worth it. A pilgrimage is more than just a holiday, it's more than just a walk it's a walk with God.

Love Beyond – The Musical

He who does not love does not know God, for God is love. 1 John 4:8

Every now and then God drops something into your life just to give you a little boost. We had regularly been listening to Premier Christian radio in the mornings when I decided to do a phone in contest, which to my amazement, I won. I had won two tickets to go to a Hillsong United concert in London. Now while I like Hillsong and have every admiration for their music and ministry, when we looked into it Hillsong United did seem to be aimed at a younger audience than ourselves and with it being in London, the expense of getting there and having to stay overnight seemed to outweigh the benefits of two free tickets to a concert we weren't exactly jumping up and down about going to (although had we gone we would have had to jump up and down). But God.

While we were still pondering whether to hand the tickets back or just go for it, we received a phone call from Premier, saying the Hillsong United concert had been cancelled, would we be willing to take two tickets for 'Love Beyond, the Musical.' We said yes and when we looked into it, it was definitely something we would want to go to.

When we got there, it was an amazing experience. We had never been at a show quite like it, as their own publicity described it, 'Love Beyond the Musical takes you on a journey beginning with the joy of creation and life, travelling through the darkness of loss and despair, and finally arriving at a place of new hope and life renewed.'

It gave the whole story from Adam to Jesus, was a completely 100% professional stage show from start to finish and God and His redemptive plan through His Son Jesus was proclaimed. That was in 2014, there was an attempt to have it tour throughout Britain, but it never came about. There was only ever two full performances at Wembley Arena and we were there. Thanks be to God.

Preaching Together. (Zacchaeus – Giving It All Away Cheerfully)

So let each one give as he purposes in his heart, not grudgingly or of necessity; for God loves a cheerful giver. 2 Corinthians 9:7

Jean and I spent two terms at North West Partnership training, a training supported by what would best be described as the more conservative evangelical churches from within the Church of England. They teach you to look into the Word of God in order to be able to teach it to others. I had had some training in this, but Jean had none. It also involved bringing a 'preach' / 'teaching' to the rest of your class group. I had preached before, Jean had never preached, ever. Every Thursday we travelled the 90-mile round trip to Leyland in Lancashire and studied the word of God with other like-minded Christians, mostly younger student type Christians. It was a challenge which we rose to and Jean especially excelled in an environment she was not used to (I had done a degree at University in a similar environment). God will get you out of your comfort zone, but He will sustain you and surprise you with what you can do.

I can do all things through Christ who strengthens me.
Philippians 4:13

One Sunday, not long after we had finished the course, we were asked to share on 'cheerful giving' at St Gabriel's in Liverpool, our then home church. St Gabriel's is a very traditional Church of England church with a faithful core of generous givers. As it should be, we had no idea who were givers and who were not. We don't pass the offering plate round as most members donate through their bank account with some through the offering plate at the back of the church. It was explained once that it wasn't proper to ask guests coming to the church to contribute to the church any more than you would ask a guest in your home to pay for a cup of tea, sounds reasonable, (megachurches take note).

Jean and I are 'tithers' a sometimes-disputed concept in traditional churches as being Old Testament, but it's something that works for us, and we were only teaching it as what we do and not as law. The following are the notes Jean and I spoke from, I varied it a little but mostly stuck to my notes, Jean has a section of testimony which she didn't write down so unfortunately that bit is missing.

Sunday 21st May 2017 - St Gabriel's Church Liverpool (Luke 19 v 1 – 10)

(Alan speaking) The heading David gave me for today was 'Cheerful giving'. Which is rather a strange talk to give a Scotsman, particularly if it relates to money. Cheerful and giving are not two words that you would expect to see crop up in the same sentence as Scotsman. But if any of you have lived in Scotland you will have found Scots to actually be very generous and forthcoming. 'They wouldnae see ye stuck.'

Scots are however very 'cannie' when it comes to money, we as a nation tend to get the most out of every pound. Something that I believe is right from the heart of God, God wants us to be good stewards of our money and getting the most out of it, and yes sometimes that means giving it away.

Zacchaeus as we see in our story was 'rich', he hadn't inherited his money and he hadn't won it on the lottery, he worked for it, it was his and he had a right to it. He was a chief tax collector and he was 'doing alright', but he knew something was missing, and that something, was about to change. Zacchaeus went looking for Jesus but to his surprise Jesus found him: when Jesus saw Zacchaeus up the tree, Jesus invited himself to Zacchaeus's house. And in verse six we see Zacchaeus hurried and came down and received Jesus joyfully.

When Jesus came to Zacchaeus's house, Zacchaeus's life was transformed, when Jesus comes into our lives things should start to change, for some instantly for others bit by bit.

With Zacchaeus it was instant, that same day, verse 8 says, Zacchaeus stood up and said to the Lord,

"Look, Lord! Here and now, I give half of my possessions to the poor, and if I have cheated anybody out of anything, I will pay back four times the amount."

Zacchaeus confesses Jesus as Lord and it's at that moment the change started. Zacchaeus not only receives Jesus, but he makes him His Lord and his eyes were opened and his priorities changed.

Jean, can you share a bit about what happened to you. (Jean went on to share about how she became a Christian and how money became unimportant, we had it all, but nothing changed, only when she made Jesus Lord of her life did it change and our attitude to money and things changed.)

JEAN... (Unfortunately, Jean doesn't read from a script so we don't have the actual words she spoke but a close paraphrase of what was said)

Like Zacchaeus we were also very well off, we were living in France, we had our own 7 apartment villa with a swimming pool, we had a large 4 x 4 and a caravan, we could go on holiday to Spain or the Pyrenees anytime we wanted, they were both only just over an hour's drive away. I didn't have to work, and Alan's shift pattern meant he had plenty of time off. It seemed like I had everything. That is why I couldn't understand what was wrong with me. Why did I feel so empty? So I started searching for answers, that's when Jesus found me.

**Salvation

– it was one day as I was ironing in our living room I was flicking through the channels on TV. We had taken Sky TV out to France with us in order that we might have some English-speaking TV to watch but never watched it much, we were usually too busy drinking and partying. This day however I was drawn to a Channel with 'GOD' up in the corner of the screen and I stopped and wondered what this was all about. There was a man on who said, 'there is someone out there who is desperate and what you need in your life is Jesus Christ.' I was drawn to the front of the TV set and got down on my knees and prayed a prayer, which we came to know as 'the sinner's prayer' a prayer of repentance and committing your life to the Lordship of Jesus, not having a clue as to what I was doing. The man said I now had to do three things, read the Bible every day, talk to Jesus every day, and join a good Bible teaching church.

I went outside to our garden, and standing by our pool I knew that things were never going to be the same again. I knew in that instant that no matter what was going to happen in the future, everything was going to be ok, even if I did have to give up all this luxury and all the material things, I still knew I had something more precious – I had met Jesus.

Then I went into our garage and somehow, in among all the boxes I managed to find the Bible we had been given on our wedding day, 17 years before, kept as a keepsake, a memento, never realising that one day it would be used to save and restore our marriage.

Alan thought I had 'flipped it.' It was going to be a long painful journey, but no pain, no gain, and we were about to gain so much more than we ever imagined....

Thank you Jean. Now that in itself is a great story but, as we'll see, it didn't end there for Jean and I and it didn't end there for Zacchaeus. This was only the beginning.

At the end of verse eight we hear Zacchaeus declaring

"Here and now, I give half of my possessions to the poor, and if I have cheated anybody out of anything, I will pay back four times the amount."

There is something very important happening here

Zacchaeus calls Jesus Lord – This is when the heart change happens.

It is only when Zacchaeus makes Jesus Lord that things start to change in his heart. You can invite Jesus into your house, but unless you invite him into your heart and make him Lord of your life, put Jesus in charge, nothing will change.

And what a change for Zacchaeus, he gives half of his goods to the poor,

Now that's a challenge, have any of you ever done that?

We did, in fact we gave away everything except the car, and within a few months we had given the car away as well. We were back in England, by this time with our teenage daughter, I had two part time jobs, one I could walk too and one on a bus route. Friends of ours lived in the country and had just had their car repossessed, they needed one, we didn't.

Zacchaeus realises that all the stuff he has, not only does he not need it, but others may be able to benefit from it. His whole attitude to what he has changes, and so should ours. Not just our attitude to things, but our attitude to money as well, and that's when God challenged me on my attitude to money, and as God so often does, when he wants to get through to a man, he will prompt his wife.

So, Jean at this stage we were relatively new Christians, you were on fire, I was getting there (slowly) and you were getting something about our giving.

Jean speaking ......

As I was learning about this new way of life, I started to talk to Jesus every day and read my Bible every day. It seemed every time I opened the Bible I ended up in the Book of Malachi, and in chapter 3 verse 8 it says

Will a man rob God? Yet you have robbed Me, But you say In what way have we robbed you? In tithes and offerings.

I had no idea what tithe meant but I did know I didn't want to be robbing God. So, the next day as I was watching the God Channel a man was speaking about tithing, he said that he gave the first 10% of all he earned to his church. I thought that this would be good for us to do too, but I would have to discuss this with Alan as he was earning all the money. I remember that day Alan and I were sitting at our kitchen table in France, I started sharing the passage from the Bible in the book of

Malachi about tithing. I suggested we could give 10% of all our earnings to the church. Alan struggled with this and seemed to be having some problems working out how much we should be giving.

Alan speaking....

It wasn't quite that straightforward, I got paid some of my salary in Francs in France at a set exchange rate and some in pounds sterling which I transferred out to France at a variable rate. I just wanted to make sure God was getting 10% (and not 10.5%) that's when Jean stepped in with 'what's so difficult you just move the point from there to there.' Maths at its simplest. Thanks Jean.

We were still in France at this time, and I was earning good money and if anyone thinks that it's alright for those with good money to tithe, they can afford it, it's simply not the case. As I said, I was earning really good money and bonuses, the day I arrived in France in 1996 I was given £10,000 just for turning up. I went straight out and bought a Toyota Landcruiser, cash. There is always a route for money no matter how much or how little you have and the route you find for money is governed by your heart. I wanted a big flashy car, I wanted to look like I had made it, and my heart was set on me.

But Jesus changed my heart, there is so much more you get from giving, not just to your church but wherever you see a need, and it is amazing how your needs seem to be met as you meet the needs of others. When we get paid, our tithe is the first thing to come off, I find when you plan to give it happens, and when you don't plan, something else crops up.

We have continued faithfully to tithe since making that decision in France, we have tithed from good wages and we have tithed off our unemployment cheque, and have never been left wanting. Our giving doesn't just stop at our tithing, it is a lifestyle and one so much more rewarding than building my own little empire.

Continuing in verse 8 we see that Zacchaeus's heart also changed towards other people. He was no longer focussed on getting as much as he could out of people, but on treating them fairly and on restoring anything he had robbed from them. When Jesus becomes our Lord, we should noticeably change. I had to lose my selfish attitude and my selfish desires, I was never going to be satisfied anyway, so why keep trying? But when you give and share what you have with others, you will be satisfied and, not only tha,t you won't have the same desire to strive after more and more.

When Zacchaeus realised all this Jesus says in Luke v 9-10

"Today salvation has come to this house, 10 For the Son of Man came to seek and to save the lost."

Salvation doesn't come to Zacchaeus's house just because Jesus turns up, any more than we become Christians when we turn up at church. Salvation comes, according to Jesus, after we make Him Lord, after we put Him in charge of our lives, and as our hearts change. Jesus doesn't just want us to invite him to be a part of our lives, to be a guest in our homes, He wants us to make Him our Lord and Saviour, He wants to change our attitudes to everything and everyone, He wants our lives to be all about Love, and He wants our lives to express that Love in every area of our lives. He wants us to have full lives, not empty self-fulfilling lives.

Steve said last week 'you can give without loving but you can't love without giving'. Let's be a people who give out of love, after all,

John 3 v 16 starts…. For God so loved the world that he gave

Amen.

It was the first time Jean and I preached in such a way and I loved it. Jean, well, let's just say she is coming round to it, while very comfortable sharing on a one to one, she still very much doesn't like sharing from the front, but it is so powerful when she does, and God honours us as we step out in faith to honour Him. We have given many (things) away but we have received so much more in its place (love, joy peace…), and best of all, the gift of eternal life through Jesus Christ.

So Jesus answered and said, "Assuredly, I say to you, there is no one who has left house or brothers or sisters or father or mother or wife or

children or lands, for My sake and the gospel's, who shall not receive a hundredfold now in this time—houses and brothers and sisters and mothers and children and lands, with persecutions—and in the age to come, eternal life. Mark 10:29-30

Weddings Galore

Therefore a man shall leave his father and mother and be joined to his wife, and they shall become one flesh. Genesis 2:24

When talking about marriage it is always good to quote God, as in the above Old Testament scripture. Which incidentally Jesus quotes in Matthew, Mark and Luke.

and said, 'For this reason a man shall leave his father and mother and be joined to his wife, and the two shall become one flesh'?
Matthew 19:5

And of course, the Apostle Paul quotes it to the Ephesians.

"For this reason a man shall leave his father and mother and be joined to his wife, and the two shall become one flesh." Ephesians 5:31

So, there can be no doubt that it is indeed God's desire that couples should become separate from their parents and form their own family. They shall become one unit, man and wife. So why do so many professing Christians think it is okay not to become man and wife but to just live together in the 'world's' standards for relationships and not God's standard?

We have come across so many that live this way and Jean has a ministry to the unwed living together and claiming to be Christians; it has been very successful. Our first challenge was our own daughter who decided that they would just live together and get married when they got around to it and had saved up some money. Well, that's another chapter (Route 33) but the final word on that was if your life together doesn't start right then tagging on a wedding day at your convenience won't be right. It won't be a 'wedding day' it will just be a day out. They got married first, praise God!

Now on the other hand if you didn't know any better when you first moved in together, i.e., you weren't Christians, then when you become Christians, the onus is on you to put it right, straight away. If we know Christians who are in error in this way then it is our duty to point it out to them and leave the Holy Spirit to work on them.

And a servant of the Lord must not quarrel but be gentle to all, able to teach, patient, in humility correcting those who are in opposition, if God perhaps will grant them repentance, so that they may know the truth, and that they may come to their senses and escape the snare of the devil, having been taken captive by him to do his will.
2 Timothy 2:24-26

Our aim in bringing people to the knowledge of God's truth is always to bring them to repentance, receive God's forgiveness, by His grace, and to see them walking in the fullness of God's light.

And you shall know the truth, and the truth shall make you free."
John 8:32

When we arrived in Liverpool there were a number of couples in the church who, to put it in 'old fashioned' terms (God's terms), were living in sin. Now everybody's correction is not the domain of one or two people but as God points them out to you and when His Holy Spirit nudges you, then you have to be obedient and bring the challenge.

We were invited round to one couple's house for dinner, a couple who we had presumed were married, they had been together a number of years and came and went to church as a 'Christian' couple dedicated to God and His ways. They talked the talk, but, as we were about to discover, weren't walking the walk. One day just before we were due to visit, we mentioned the woman by the man's surname and were told, oh that's not her name, they aren't married.

We went round to their house and during the meal Jean challenged them on it and while they were trying to explain why they weren't married and how they came to be living together, we believe the Holy

Spirit was working in them and that their excuses were beginning to sound to them as hollow as they did to God. They didn't however commit to doing anything about it. Jean quoted them the scripture:

Immorality Must Be Judged

I wrote to you in my epistle not to keep company with sexually immoral people. 10 Yet I certainly did not mean with the sexually immoral people of this world, or with the covetous, or extortioners, or idolaters, since then you would need to go out of the world. 11 But now I have written to you not to keep company with anyone named a brother, who is sexually immoral, or covetous, or an idolater, or a reviler, or a drunkard, or an extortioner—not even to eat with such a person. 1 Corinthians 5:9-11

Later that year they went on holiday and came back engaged. Now this to them was a step in the right direction but really it was just a confirmation that they were 'living in sin' but were not married. It took a long while for them eventually to get married, but they have now been obedient to God and the promptings of the Holy Spirit and are living as God intended. Not only are we free to eat with them, but they are involved in ministering with us. God has set them free to do what He has called them to do which is minister from within the body of Christ and not minister as Satan would have them do, running about outwith the church and being easy targets for Him.

Blessed Unity of the People of God A Song of Ascents. Of David. Behold, how good and how pleasant it is For brethren to dwell together in unity! Psalm 133:1

The next couple who we had been speaking to were 'older' as well. He had also been coming along to church since before we arrived and was quite a prominent member of the community. A previous relationship had collapsed, and he was now very friendly with the new love of his life and they were attending church regularly. After a few years, they moved in together, it just made sense, to whom? Certainly not God, and as friends of theirs and members of God's family together, Jean challenged them on this. They took it on board and one Sunday Jean asked them well, when's the big day? They said Easter, they had decided to get married and were looking at around Easter time, and it was exciting, but Church. God's plan is for His people to be married and when a couple decide to do this then they should be able to do so. But apparently, as I put it, divorce is the unpardonable sin.

Therefore, if anyone is in Christ, he is a new creation; old things have passed away; behold, all things have become new. 2 Corinthians 5:17

She was a widow and so no problem with that, but he had been divorced, many years earlier, and so the Church of England would not marry them until He went through a series of, I don't know what, but anyway he said no. That was all in his past and he was now a Christian, he was forgiven and if the Church of England wouldn't marry them, he would just go elsewhere, which they did. How sad that when someone decides to do the right thing in God's eyes they are rejected and humiliated by the Church to such an extent that they feel the need to go elsewhere. While the Church of England are in discussions over marrying same sex couples, we are putting off mature heterosexual couples who want to get married and sending them to the world to oversee it. Where, incidentally, there are strict rules about keeping God out of the ceremony. They came back to the church but after a while have drifted away, we are praying for them to return but who knows what deep hurts they have against a church which refused them the right to get married in the House of God.

Incidentally, the first couple I mentioned also had to get married outside of the Church for the same reason. He had been married before and divorced so they couldn't get married in the Church. She however hadn't been married before but had lived with and had a child to another man, but that was okay, as long as she hadn't been married. How hypocritical is that? She could be accepted because she had lived by the world's standards, but he couldn't because he had lived by God's standards. Now I know God hates divorce, but surely repentance is followed by forgiveness and old things have passed away and a new start is offered. A new start which feels like freedom and not condemnation.

Free from Indwelling Sin

8 There is therefore now no condemnation to those who are in Christ Jesus, who do not walk according to the flesh, but according to the Spirit. Romans 8:1

Now the third wedding I am going to talk about confirms the absurdity of the above two. This couple had never been married before. He had had long term live-in relationships, he never had any children in them but did become a father figure to step-children. She had been in a long term relationship with a man to whom she had a child. When they decided to get married to each other there was no problem, they had a church wedding and were made to feel they were doing the right thing before God. Old things had passed away and they were free to marry. This to me confirms the world's view that marriage is just a piece of paper. If you don't have the piece of paper you are free, if you do have the piece of paper you are condemned, not by God, but certainly by the Church of England.

She was an alcoholic, had come to us for help and support and had become a Christian. She was coming to church when she met this nice 'Christian' man. They were soon dating and after some time it became apparent that they were more than dating, she became pregnant. Jean challenged them on this and in no uncertain terms the man let her know he was not getting married; he couldn't do it. He said he couldn't stand up in front of all those people. Jean said there doesn't have to be a lot of people, you are doing it before God not man. To cut a long story short they got married. It was a small candlelight service one evening in the church with just close family and of course God. It was the most God focussed wedding we have been at. It was only happening because they wanted God at the centre of their marriage and not because they wanted a day out, it was wonderful. They now have two children and God has helped and supported them through difficult times, times which I believe had they not been married and made that commitment before God, they would not have got through and would have given up on each other. But they are now part of a Kingdom that does not give up on people and encourages us not to give up on each other either. Praise God.

This is an ongoing ministry for us, and in particular Jean, who God has gifted with the grace to bring these challenges and see results, but there is one more story I would like to share.

This couple came to the church to have their fourth child baptised, and he decided that he liked it so much that he was coming back, which they all say, but this time this man meant it. He knew God was calling to him and he wanted to know what it was all about. They came along for several months and when we found out they weren't married, Jean challenged them about it. There was no particular reason that they weren't married; they had just never got around to it. They had been together since they were teenagers, over thirty years. After a while, she began not coming to church, various excuses but none that held any water, he however was steadfast in his walk. He was reading his Bible, studying the word, and helping out at the foodbank and anywhere else in the church he could.

One Sunday Jean was prompted by the Holy Spirit to say to him 'If you ask her to marry you, she will come back to church'. He never said much. A couple of weeks later he took Jean aside and said, 'She said, yes.' After thirty-six years of living together they were getting married. Again, it was a wonderful occasion as it was being done unto the Lord.

We have another couple we are been working on, nudged by the Holy Spirit, but they are harder work. When you don't have that relationship with God through the Holy Spirit then the conviction of the Spirit isn't there and therefore the desire to be in right relationship with God through obedience to His Word is not a priority. You will get around to doing it one day, but as I said to my daughter that isn't a wedding, it's a day out, where you are the priority, not God. We keep praying for them that they will both be filled with the Spirit and get the revelation of God's plan for their lives and their relationship. They have recently come along to our Sunday @ 6 group and are growing in their faith and praise God they will get married soon and walk in the fullness of what God has planned for them.

For I know the plans I have for you,' declares the Lord, 'plans to prosper you and not to harm you, plans to give you hope and a future.
Jeremiah 29:11 (NIVUK)

If you are a 'Christian' couple living together and not married and you ever come across us, and in particular Jean, remember we love you and we want God's best for you. Therefore, we will challenge you, in Jesus name. Amen.

58

Crosshouse

*Now all who believed were together, and had all things in common,
and sold their possessions and goods, and divided them among all, as
anyone had need. Acts 2:44-45*

In 2016 I had a vision for a house where we would live and support
people coming out of chaotic lifestyles. I had a particular house in
mind, it was owned by the Church of England who were selling it but,
so the story goes, being a charity, they had to sell it to the highest
bidder. Our backer was not the highest bidder and couldn't raise any
more money, so we lost that house. Incidentally, the house was next
to a Christian pre-school which is now run by a secular charity, and a
Christian youth centre, which is now over seen by a secular charity.
Although the youth centre now accommodates a church, not a Church
of England Church but at least it's a Christian Church. The Church of
England is losing ground and seems to be retreating into 'comfortable'
'nice' Sunday morning churches where all are welcome and repentance
(Jesus used it all the time) is not part of their vocabulary. The Devil is
having a field day. Incidentally, while editing this in 2020 I can confirm
that both buildings, the pre-school and the youth centre, have been
closed as unsafe and not fit for purpose, what is God saying in that?

*And Jesus answered and said to them, "Do you suppose that these
Galileans were worse sinners than all other Galileans, because they
suffered such things? I tell you, no; but unless you repent you will all
likewise perish. Or those eighteen on whom the tower in Siloam fell
and killed them, do you think that they were worse sinners than all
other men who dwelt in Jerusalem? I tell you, no; but unless you
repent you will all likewise perish." Luke 13:2-5*

The following is our vision for 'Crosshouse' which we have laid down, for the time being. It may have been the wrong house, it may have been the wrong time, or it may not even be from God. But should God put it in our hearts again we are ready to lift it up and run with it. We have a full partner pack prepared, of which the vision section is just a small part.

Crosshouse Vision

We are looking to identify a property in the area with at least five bedrooms which we would look to take on as a safe environment for adults looking to be set free from chaotic lifestyles, who have made a clear indication of a desire to change (e.g., from rehabs, prisons, abusive relationship, etc.) We are keen to support people like ex-offenders and ex-addicts who have made a commitment to Christ and are looking to continue in their journey with Christ while readjusting to life, helping and supporting them to reintegrate into the community. We are looking at offering short term supported accommodation (3-6 months). We would be offering a room in a shared house with a live-in support couple.

The vision is to call it Crosshouse, and while living there, residents would be expected to participate in:

1.) Crosslife, a Christ centred, Bible based discipleship programme.

2.) Crosswork, working in the community doing jobs like gardening, furniture restoration, car wash, etc. We are looking to develop this into paid work as small business enterprises, initially working from the house and perhaps eventually opening a shop.

3.) Crossreach, outreach into the community helping at such outreaches as Foodbank, and Foodhub, drawing on the experience of the individuals to speak to others about the difference Christ has made to their lives. The discipleship programme would be compulsory for all residents but also be open to the general public. We are looking at basing it on the Celebrate Recovery model which is a Christ centred, Biblically based 12 step program, and redoing it to meet our specific needs. We have had interest in this from people who we have met through the foodbank and foodhub.

Sunday would be church with an afternoon service in order that we may draw help and support from surrounding churches, particularly in worship. We would be open to Crosshouse becoming their church or, as they grew in their faith, they would be able to start attending a church of their choice. We would be looking to the church they attend to assist in the support and ongoing discipleship of the person.

We see the house as being targeted at people who have already made a start in their Christian walk and who just need that extra bit of support when trying to establish their own permanent accommodation. We are looking at a maximum of 6 months in order that we may be able to help as many people as possible, but this would not be rigid.

As well as disciple them in the Christian faith we would be offering practical help, debt advice, cooking skills, budgeting, and offering ongoing support from the house when they move back into the local community.

A Ponytail

Does not even nature itself teach you that if a man has long hair, it is a dishonour to him? 1 Corinthians 11:14

I usually use the above scripture in a light-hearted way to show that Paul was bald. Obviously to him nature's gift of hair taught him that men couldn't grow long hair while women could. However, while nature teaches some men that, for others nature teaches us that we can quite easily grow long hair just the same as women can, and if you add in a long hairy beard then actually men are more able to cover their head (and faces) with more hair than your average woman. I had always thought ponytails on men looked quite ridiculous, as a fashion statement or any other statement it didn't work for me.

Judging others
'Do not judge, or you too will be judged. Matthew 7:1 (NIVUK)

So, when my hair had become long and unmanageable, Jean said to me 'You should put it in a ponytail'. Well, that just wasn't going to happen. I had stopped going to the barbers for whatever reason (probably because they wanted £10 a go) and had been unsuccessfully cutting my own hair for a while (Jean refused and said I should get it done properly) and now I had ended up just doing nothing with it. Before I knew it, it had become long and, as I said, unmanageable. Then one day I put it in a small ponytail, just in the house you understand, and it worked. Gradually I became bolder and bolder to the point where I wore a ponytail to church, and we're not talking a short ponytail, we are talking three years' of growth ponytail.

Then it happened, Jean had made an appointment at a newly opened hairdressers in the Dingle. She was going to get highlights and decided to give the girl some business, but as it happened a girl in the church who does Jean's hair said she could do highlights for Jean at home, so Jean said ok, and she still does Jean's hair to this day. However, Jean felt bad about having to cancel the appointment especially as it was a new start business, so she said to me 'Why don't you take my appointment?' Now I hadn't become a Nazarite,

whose head is never to be touched by a razor because the boy is to be a Nazirite, dedicated to God. Judges 13:5 (NIVUK)

Therefore, I wasn't under any oath or covenant re my hair, and it was needing tidied up, so I went.

I said to the girl 'My wife had an appointment with you, but she can't make it'. She said that's okay, escape time, no, we felt it right to keep our commitment to this hairdresser so I said, 'Can I have her appointment?' She said 'Yes, what do you want done?' I said I didn't know. When I sat down on the chair I just said 'Cut it off', she said 'All of it?' I said yes. When my hair was washed, she said 'Are you sure?' And I said yes, and that was the end of my ponytail.

When I got home, Jean was quite shocked that I had been so drastic but ah well. You know what they say, 'Hair today, gone tomorrow.'

At this moment in time my hair is growing long again, and I can just manage a short ponytail to keep it reasonably tidy, but it's that time again when you have to grin and bear it and push on through, or cut it off, we'll see. Paul says, 'Cut it', the angel of the Lord says, 'Dedicate it to God'.

you are not under the law, but under grace. Romans 6:14 (NIVUK)

We All – Song Number Two. (You Have to Sing It or Say It With A Texan Drawl)

Sing to Him a new song; Play skilfully with a shout of joy. Psalm 33:3

This was the second song I got from the Lord and sums up pretty much how I feel about Sunday morning Christianity and how we need to be living the Christian life to those around us seven days a week.

We all look so good on Sunday
We all sing so sweet on Sunday
We all smile at the preacher on Sunday
But Jesus didn't come for all of that.

We all curse our boss on Monday
We all shout at the kids on Tuesday
We all go to the pub on Wednesday
We all tip a dollar to the homeless on Thursday
We all scream and shout its Friday
We all shop till we drop on Saturday
But Jesus didn't come for all of that.

We all look so good on Sunday
We all sing so sweet on Sunday
We all smile at the preacher on Sunday
But Jesus didn't come for all of that.

We all should preach the Gospel on Monday
We all should heal the sick on Tuesday
We all should disciple them on Wednesday
We all should mend the broken hearted on Thursday

We all should set the captives free on Friday
We all should love your neighbour on Saturday
Because Jesus came for all of that.

Then we all would see the Spirit move on Sunday
We all would sing and dance on Sunday
We all would Praise the Lord on Sunday
Because Jesus. He came for all of that.

Axel – Two Holes in The Heart

And Jesus went about all Galilee, teaching in their synagogues, preaching the gospel of the kingdom, and healing all kinds of sickness and all kinds of disease among the people. Matthew 4:23

After three miscarriages and a painful C-section to have their first child it was quite a surprise to hear that Kerry was now pregnant again. Immediately a lot of prayer started happening. Nine months later in January 2018 they had another baby boy. Axel Robert Kettle, Robert being the name of Jean's brother, Kerry's uncle, who had committed suicide. As for Axel, well that certainly wasn't in the Bible right? Well wrong actually.

The name Axel is the Scandinavian and German form of the old Biblical name Absalom. Absalom in turn is derived from the Hebrew name Avshalom which means "my father is peace". So it is a Hebrew name, and while Absalom's story in the Bible doesn't end well, I say Amen to the Hebrew meaning of his name 'my father is peace'. Axel's father is the Prince of Peace and the King of Kings, the Lord God Himself, his very own 'Father in Heaven'.

The very first time in hospital I held Axel, I felt there was something not right and said so, I laid my hand on his tiny little chest and prayed for him. Shortly afterwards the doctor gave us the news that he had two holes in his heart, a small one which they weren't concerned with, and a larger one which they said they would have to keep an eye on and would probably need a procedure done on it. But God. Jean and I believed that God had shown me this and that when I laid hands on Axel he was healed. We kept praying and believing.

...they will lay hands on the sick, and they will recover." Mark 16:18

A few months later Kerry came home from a hospital check-up for Axel with the news 'the large hole in the heart was gone' and they expected the small one to heal as well, Amen to that. It was such a relief, but God was definitely answering prayer. Now I know Kerry and Andrew and many others will ask the question, why did they have to go through three miscarriages? And why did Axel have two holes in his heart in the first place? There are no answers to that but all I know is that God can be trusted, and He loves each and every one of us.

The latest update on Axel is that his heart is completely normal, praise God from whom al blessings flow.

Trust in the Lord with all your heart, And lean not on your own understanding; Proverbs 3:5

Camino de Portuguese – Fatima

The Joy of Going to the House of the Lord A Song of Ascents. Of
David.
*I was glad when they said to me, "Let us go into the house of the
Lord."* Psalm 122:1

It was 2018 and we had the 'Camino bug'. We had been so exhilarated
by the Camino de Santiago experience we did a short Camino in 2015
but it never felt quite like a pilgrimage, then we came across the
Camino de Portuguese, it ran from Lisbon to Santiago via Porto. We
were never going to attempt it from Lisbon (380 miles) but from Porto
(140 miles) it looked possible. As we investigated it, we found that
there were direct flights from Liverpool (where we were currently
living) to Porto and started making plans to walk it that summer.

Again, just like the first Camino, we had a great time. Walk, Eat, Sleep,
repeat for fourteen days doesn't sound much like fun but it's more
than fun it as an amazing spiritual experience. God is with you and you
can feel His presence, His guidance and His love every step of the way.
It was the first time we had been in Portugal and loved the people and
the place, it was so peaceful and simple a lifestyle as we walked north
of Porto through some wonderful countryside and small villages. As in
Spain each village has a small but wonderful church in its midst, and
even many of their gardens contain images of Jesus, Mary and crosses.

Once, while passing through a small village, we were desperate for a
rest, the walking was taking its toll, but God was sustaining us. We saw
a small church, but the front door was closed as was the side door. As
we stood there an old woman approached Jean and motioned that we
had to go round the other side. She was standing beside an old,

abandoned building not really doing anything. We went round the other side of the building and went in through the door, there stood a statue of Jesus with His arms outstretched to welcome us. After a short stay and some prayer, we were revived enough to continue on our pilgrimage. As we stepped outside, there was no sign of the old lady and as we looked at where she had been standing, we couldn't figure out why she would even be standing there. God had sent an angel.

While we were walking through Portugal heading for Santiago in Spain, we had come across blue arrows going in the opposite direction than the yellow arrows we were following. It was a route to Fatima. The seed was sown. When we returned, Jean started investigating Fatima and we decided it would be something we would like to do. The next year we ended up at Fatima.

We flew out from Liverpool again to Porto, got a bus into the city and then another onto Fatima from where we planned to walk back to Porto following part of the Camino de Santiago section from Lisbon to Porto, about 120 miles. We would walk as much as we were comfortable with. When we walked into the Shrine of Our Lady of Fatima, the presence and peace of God were there. It was early evening, very calm and we could hear the Mass being sung in at open air service within the grounds. Whatever your views of Roman Catholic adoration of Mary and shrines to 'Our Lady' I challenge you to go to a place like the Shrine of Our Lady of Fatima and say they are doing something wrong. The reverence for God in the place and the love of Jesus is so overwhelming that you cannot deny God is honoured and glorified by all that is going on. We returned the following evening for the candlelit Mass and again it just takes your breath away to see so many thousands of people sitting and standing around with candles taking Mass in the open air, it was beautiful.

The next day we started our walk to Porto the first leg from Fatima to Tomar, not part of the Camino de Santiago but the shortest (?) way to connect with the Camino. We started off early in the morning and as we set off, I saw in the distant horizon the Castle at Tomar. After walking for a few hours, the Castle had disappeared away behind us. We had been walking and walking and when we crossed under the main road, I saw a sign for Tomar saying 25K, it was only supposed to be 27K from Fatima and we had already been walking all morning. I checked google and, yes, we had been heading northeast and not directly east and were now north of Tomar. I couldn't work out how to get on the Camino at any other point, so we kept walking and praying heading for Tomar. We entered a small village, everywhere was shut, it was Sunday afternoon. We saw an old Mercedes taxi sitting at the side of the road. You never see taxis in rural villages, it was parked opposite a closed looking café bar, but the door was slightly ajar. We decided to go in and ask if they knew the taxi driver. He was sitting inside the café bar with what looked like some family. I asked him if he could take us to Tomar and how much it would be. We agreed a price and set off. We could never have walked that distance. As we entered Tomar there was a huge festival on and cars queued and parked everywhere. It was the "Festa dos Tabuleiros", something that only happens every four years and we were there right at the right time. Praise God.

We got stuck in traffic and the meter was ticking around and around and I said to Jean let's get out and walk. She said I can't walk another step, she spoke to our Portuguese drive who assured us that we had agreed a price and that is all he would charge, and may God bless his business. We didn't have any accommodation booked for that night and there were people everywhere, Jean got on booking.com and got us a hotel, we had no idea where it was in Tomar, but it was a room. The driver dropped us off next to the Convent of Christ, the hilltop 'castle' I had seen early that morning. We walked through the grounds and down into the town and quickly found our hotel. It was right in the centre of the old town, some of the streets were decorated with hanging paper flower arrangements, and our hotel was in one of these streets. It was an amazing blessing and the grace of God. The procession was spectacular and the streets full, five or six deep, for hours beforehand, these people had to be staying somewhere but we had our room handy for everything.

The next morning, we were due to set off, we were on the Camino de Santiago now and ready to start walking in the right direction, but before we left, we seen some commotion at the far end of the main street and headed up to see what was happening. There were two sets of two bulls yoked to two carts. While we watched, Jean got too close for a photograph and was promptly warned not to get too close. A local Portuguese girl started talking to Jean, apparently one of the bulls had got a bit upset and smashed one of the carts to pieces, 'There is nothing you can do with an angry bull' she said. The carts take bread and wine round the streets to be given out to the needy. The bread and wine representing the sacrifice of Christ.

We headed off and spent the next few days walking to Porto, just outside the city of Porto itself we boarded a bus for the last stage. We met an American couple who were walking from Lisbon to Santiago and were also getting the bus. The walking from Lisbon was proving challenging, they also had previously walked the Camino Frances and were struggling with the surroundings they were walking. We were able to share that we had completed the next stage from Porto to Santiago and it was more like the rural walking they had come to appreciate on the Camino Frances. Jean also shared testimony with them and advised them on the wisdom God had given her for blisters and knees. We arrived back in Porto and had a nice meal in a local tavern, headed out to the airport for a night's rest then back to Liverpool. Refreshed and blessed.

The Lord Calls...

A third time the LORD called, 'Samuel!' And Samuel got up and went to Eli and said, 'Here I am; you called me.' Then Eli realised that the LORD was calling the boy. So Eli told Samuel, 'Go and lie down, and if he calls you, say, "Speak, LORD, for your servant is listening."' So Samuel went and lay down in his place. The LORD came and stood there, calling as at the other times, 'Samuel! Samuel!' Then Samuel said, 'Speak, for your servant is listening.' 1 Samuel 3:8-10 (NIVUK)

In June 2018 we were working as evangelists and community outreach workers in St Gabriel's Church, Liverpool. We had been there just over four years under David Gavin our minister and line manager when he announced that he was moving to a new parish, still in Liverpool, and would be moving at the end of August. David had been our main prayer support during our time at St Gabriel's, meeting with us twice a week and he was concerned that we would not have this when he left, to this end he introduced us to Bill and his wife Alice. Bill and Alice were immediately a blessing to us, and we were just instantly comfortable with each other. After only a few meetings in September 2018, Bill said to us, 'I'm not saying this is from the Lord or anything, but have you considered ordination?'

Since I first became a Christian, I have always felt called to ministry of some sort. In 2000 while living in France my Anglican minister Rev Laurie Mort came round to see me and said he felt that God had a call on my life, he didn't know whether it would be in the Church of England or the Church of Scotland but said there was a definite call on my life. I was in the process of giving up my job and going to a Bible college in England and I took this word to be that I was on the right track, completely ignoring the fact that it wasn't run by a mainstream denomination.

Sometime later we moved back to Scotland, while there we went to the local Church of Scotland church. After being there some time, our minister came to see me and said he felt that I had a call on my life and had I ever thought about the ministry? I ended up going through the selection process with the Church of Scotland, I also started studying at the University of Glasgow. After a year I was turned down for selection, I accepted that but finished my degree. Both my minister and the minister I had been with for six months suggested I try again but I didn't.

Now our new minister friend was saying have you ever considered ordination?' I had said I thought I was too old to be considered, certainly by Church of Scotland guidelines I am. But I committed to pray about it. That week while driving home I burst into the song 'The Leaving of Liverpool', not a song I am particularly familiar with, in fact I only know it from the 80's when my friend had a collection of Dubliners cassette tapes. Jean asked me 'Where did that come from?' I had no idea. As we drove home, I noticed Jo's car at the church, Jo was someone we had met during our time at St Gabriel's at that time he had a small workshop in the church basement, I don't know how Jo would refer to himself but without meaning any offence I would say he was 'an old hippy'. Jo is just different in a nice and good way, an individual, which is the way God made us all, anyway. I dropped Jean of and went to see Jo. He was just leaving the church basement and had a painting of a tall ship on a piece of wood, he was going to take it to a mutual friend who was in the hospital he said, 'I'm going to put 'The Leaving of Liverpool' on it, do you know that song?' I said I was just singing it five minutes ago. That Saturday evening, we were at a show called 'Lost and Found' a retelling of the parable of the prodigal son, featuring the Sanctuary Soul Gospel Choir. Three songs in, they stopped and a three-piece ukulele band came in singing 'The Leaving of Liverpool', it was totally out of context with what we were expecting and the third time I had now heard this song.

Next morning my first daily reading was 1 Samuel 3 with the heading 'The Lord calls Samuel'. I knew straight away that God called Samuel three times before he realised it was God. I had had the song three times, so God had my attention on the 'three times', but more importantly I realised that it was now the third time God had used a man of God to speak to me about ordination, I decided it was right to test this call.

Later that week I was reading Matthew and about the Angel of the Lord speaking in dreams. I decided to ask God for a dream; that night I dreamt that I was having a phone call with someone who was saying he wasn't putting me forward for ministry despite the fact I had everything they were looking for. God spoke to me and said that man may reject me, but He never will. I took that as encouragement not to look at my previous application for selection with the Church of Scotland, but to carry on with this and apply to the Church of England for ordination.

I eventually withdrew from the ordination process as I felt it wasn't right for me and that it was not what God was calling me to. The dream I had about getting a phone call from someone who said I was not being put forward for ordination, maybe that was God. The man's name was Colin, I don't know, and have yet to meet, someone called Colin, perhaps it was God 'calling'.

As for the leaving of Liverpool? Well, we are fairly comfortable here and maybe I wasn't ready to listen to God saying we were leaving Liverpool. We must always be careful how we interpret things from God; even when it is from God, we can still interpret it with our own slant. Very dangerous. In 2019 our church building was a building site and very difficult to work from and now in 2020 we find ourselves unable to access the building again due to Lockdown and the new initiatives we started at the beginning of the year are closed. Maybe I just need to take a simple interpretation of 'The Leaving of Liverpool' and get ready to leave Liverpool, in a new and exciting journey with God. God doesn't do comfortable, and neither do Jean and I, we want to wear out and not rust out.

Priesthood?

But you are a chosen generation, a royal priesthood, a holy nation, His own special people, that you may proclaim the praises of Him who called you out of darkness into His marvellous light; 1 Peter 2:9

As part of investigating and testing my call to ordination I was asked to look at my understanding of Priesthood and particularly Priesthood within the Church of England. Being from the West of Scotland and brought up in a 'them and us' culture (them being the Catholics and us being the proddys, - that's Protestants) my understanding was Catholics had Priests, we had ministers and never the twain shall meet. Here is my short reflection on the subject.

Readings:

The Widening Circle - Graham Tomlin

The Christian Priest Today – Michael Ramsey

All Things Anglican – Marcus Troup

Self-Supporting Ministry –John Lees

Faith Confirmed, preparing for confirmation – Peter Jackson and Chris Wright

Common Worship Ordination Service – Church of England.org

'Priests are called to be servants and shepherds among people to whom they are sent.' This is a quote from the ordination service for Priests in the Church of England and very much resonates with what I feel called to and to a great extent is what I do already. But does that mean I am called to be a pries?, In many ways we are all called to be priests and I believe in the priesthood of the believers, so what is so specific about being called to the 'office' of priest?

Graham Tomlin in his book *The Widening Circle* talks about the various levels of priesthood, from the priesthood of all which we are 'ordained' into as such through Baptism, the priesthood as a specific ministry, and the High Priesthood of Christ, who is our ultimate example of servant and shepherd. Graham puts it like this, "Ordination is not a commissioning for ministry, but a setting apart for a particular kind of ministry." So, I believe I am called to ministry as we all are, but am I being called to be set apart for this particular kind of ministry? And if so, is my understanding of 'this kind of ministry' the same as The Church of England's?

I was brought up in the Church of Scotland, went away from it and, at the age of 40, I met Jesus, became a Christian and went to an Anglican Church. My options at the time were limited. I was living in France and it was the only English-speaking church I knew of, in fact it was called 'The English Speaking Church of Toulouse'. I had no problem being part of it and felt the general feel to it as being similar to the Church of Scotland. Many years later I have ended up in Liverpool, where I have been for the last five years, working in the Church of England. It was this more in-depth meeting with the Church of England and its ways that lead me to see a whole new language and culture. Terms like Curate, Vicar, PCC, DCC, and in particular the term Priest, were new to me. Where I grew up the term priest referred to the Catholic Priest, we had a minister, and the priest would inevitably be Irish. Perhaps a little typecast but definitely true in the West of Scotland. So, to be looking at the term Priesthood in such a way as being called to it is extremely strange. The New Testament writers obviously felt the same as they avoid the term when talking about offices in the new church, using the term mainly to refer back to the Old Testament ways but also as a reference to Christ the High Priest.

So, what is the term referring to in the Church of England? Do I resonate with this understanding? And does this understanding tie in with my calling from God?

The *Ordination Service for Priesthood* goes on to talk about the responsibility of the priest as being:

to tell the story of God's love.

Baptize new disciples in the name of the Father, and of the Son, and of the Holy Spirit.

walk with them in the way of Christ, nurturing them in the faith.

to unfold the Scriptures.

to preach the word in season and out of season.

to declare the mighty acts of God.

to preside at the Lord's table.

lead his people in worship, offering with them a spiritual sacrifice of praise and thanksgiving.

to bless the people in God's name.

to resist evil, support the weak, defend the poor, and intercede for all in need.

to minister to the sick and prepare the dying for their death.

Guided by the Spirit, they are to discern and foster the gifts of all God's people that the whole Church may be built up in unity and faith.

Looking at each of these, there is a great responsibility in Priesthood and as such a great responsibility in making sure that it is God's calling and that it is not a vain desire to be recognised but a humble desire to serve. I already serve in many of the above areas within the Church of England in my role as evangelist and community outreach worker, and the leading of our Sunday night group in the church. I am now seeking God's will as to the calling on my life.

In ministering to people as I do there is nothing really that I am doing that we are not all called to do as the body of Christ, other than I have given my whole life to it since becoming a Christian. I left full time employment in 2000, sold my home and, with my family, headed off to

Bible college. It would be 2014 before I would have another full-time job and it would be in ministry here in Liverpool. In all that time God was faithful and provided for our every need, we never had the big house, nice car or the same access to all the material things we previously had, but we have had peace and joy and today are completely blessed in our new life in Christ. I have reached the stage in my life (60 this year) where being ordained is not a career step and, in many ways I am bemused at why I am even looking at going through such a long process when I am more than happy where I am. But something inside me keeps urging me on and whatever the outcome I believe in investigating this feeling of calling, believing that God, through his Spirit, will do something new.

So, I see priesthood as God's plan for His Church, not just the priesthood of all the saints but a specific priesthood of a specific people called by God himself. Graham Tomlin talks in his book *The Widening Circle* of the way God works in using the part to bless the whole. "God uses humanity (the part) to bless Creation (the whole), He uses the Church (the part) to bless Humanity (the whole), and He uses the Priest (the part) to bless the Church (the whole)."

I believe God is calling me to be the part (the priest) that blesses the whole (the church). I believe that is within the context of where God has called me at this time, the Church of England.

While looking at priesthood I also looked at the Church of England and the Anglican Communion. I read through *All Things Anglican* by Marcus Throup and found no checks in my spirit with it.

The Church of England is a vast and complex organisation with many different strands and views, but so has humanity. My encouragement is in Throup's summing up of the Essentials of Anglican Theology where he states three characteristics. First, Anglican Theology is Christ Centred; Second, it is Trinity shaped; and thirdly it is Spirit Fuelled. Amen.

Having come from a different tradition, the Church of Scotland, I have recently gone through confirmation with the Church of England and was confirmed on the 23rd June 2019 by the laying on of hands of

Bishop Bev. The preparation for my confirmation has helped deepen my understanding of what it means to be a Christian in the Church of England but also first and foremost what it means to be a Christian in the worldwide Church of Christ.

I look forward to continuing my journey in testing the call and will of God for my life.

Alan McKinnell

2nd July 2019.

Kerry – Our Blessing

Children are a gift from the Lord; they are a real blessing.
Psalm 127:3 (GNT)

Probably Kerry would be the best person to write this chapter as only she really knows how she felt and what she made of things in her upbringing. From the party lifestyle of her parents, to the moving of houses, schools and even countries. From money grabbing parents who provided her with a home with a pool to the Christian parents who uprooted her again and took her to a rented house where she once again knew no one and had to start again. New country (England), new home, new school, new friends a lot for a now teenager. When we were drinkers there were always people around and they usually had children as well so our friend's children became Kerry's friends, friends of circumstance not of choice. Many children will find this but interestingly, many years later when Kerry got married none of these children were her close friends. She had four bridesmaids, her two cousins, a friend from Horsham and a friend from University, she also had a friend from France come over to the UK for her wedding. Gone were the friends of circumstance. I don't know what this has to do with anything, but it just struck me.

Kerry was cared for and looked after and Jean didn't go straight back to work when she could have, despite it being a well-paid supervisor's role in Marks and Spencer's. When Jean eventually did go back to work it wasn't at M and S with a view to the money but always wherever the hours would suit being there for Kerry. I, however, do not really recall being there for Kerry. I was involved in work and drinking and how much quality time did I give her? I doubt it was much.

We moved when Kerry was age seven from our village to the town of Ayr where Kerry went to a new school. She settled in well, was a popular pupil and she attended Brownies where she got the Brownie of the year award. Then at the age of nine we took her to live in France. Following the advice given to us by the resettling office and those who had 'been there and done that', we put Kerry in a French speaking village school where it was sink or swim. She had no French but learned quickly and well and made some French friends. By the time we were leaving France she was fourteen; moving a teenager anywhere is challenging but moving from France back to England well, I really don't know how much we discussed it with her, I was going to Bible college in West Sussex and that was that. One thing we did discuss was that she was going to an all-girls school, another completely new concept to Kerry and us. She always got on well and made small groups of friends and was never any trouble for us. We were there two years before moving again to Lincolnshire and this time a grammar school. While we did get the teenage rebellion stage, she did well at school and went to University, all this is discussed in another chapter.

The upstart of it all is that we have been truly blessed by an amazing daughter who has been a great blessing to us. She went through such a lot in her school years and came out on top. We are still part of her life and she is a good wife to Andrew and a great mum to our two grandsons, Rufus and Axel.

Relationships are a constant work, and we pray and seek God that we will always be a part of their lives and that it will continue to be a joy. This December we are taking all the family to Lapland for an early start to Christmas before coming home to concentrate on the real meaning of Christmas, the birth of our Lord and Saviour Jesus Christ.

One day maybe Kerry will reveal all she went through, a lot of it was tough and a lot of it a mess, but God is good, and we are still standing as a family by the grace of God. We love Kerry dearly and are proud of the young woman she is, and the gift she has given us in grandsons.

Children's children are the crown of old men, Proverbs 17:6

And The Story Continues…. Get Your Kicks

So when they had brought their boats to land, they forsook all and followed Him. Luke 5:11

As I write this, we are preparing to visit Toulouse where we became Christians, it is the first time we will have visited there since leaving in September 2000, 19 years ago. We have no idea what to expect but it is amazing that at the time I write the last chapter of this book God has us on our way to where the first chapter of our Christian life began, more than 20 years ago. The day we return from France will be my 60th birthday and on arrival back in the UK will be going out for a meal with Kerry Andrew and the boys. I will be reflecting on how differently my 60th birthday could have turned out, if I had seen it, and thanking God all day for my wonderful wife who stood by me and the blessings that have unfolded in my life through God's grace and Jean's faithfulness (to me and to God). Our Route 66, the sixty-six books of the Bible, our road map to life, promises to take us on even greater adventures. Just yesterday morning I lay face down on the floor after my quiet time (something I don't do enough of) and I believe God spoke to me saying, 'Enjoy Toulouse but I have a greater journey ahead for you and Jean. You will not need to go to Egypt for your provision.'

I look forward to that greater journey, the journey of life with Jesus as Lord. And whatever the provision God is talking about, I thank Him for it now and receive it in the name of Jesus. All will be revealed in God's timing. If your Christian journey is not exciting (and challenging) I would ask you, are you doing it right? Are you being obedient? Jean and I often say our Christian life has been everything but boring.

The folly of not trusting God
*Woe to those who go down to Egypt for help, And rely on horses, Who
trust in chariots because they are many, And in horsemen because
they are very strong, But who do not look to the Holy One of Israel,
Nor seek the Lord!* Isaiah 31:1

Toulouse 2019 – age 60

On Monday the 16th September 2019 we flew out to Toulouse for five
days, it had been arranged for several months. It happened when we
were in Portugal on our latest pilgrimage and I said to Jean I would like
to go back to Toulouse for my sixtieth birthday. To begin with I was
thinking of driving all over the place including to Santiago and Fatima
and Lourdes and then I thought, I don't really want to do that I just
want to go back to Toulouse where I had become a Christian twenty
years ago. Jean was really excited about the idea I never knew it had
been a dream of hers to go back there one day. It was going to be a
special one-off occasion.

Nine days before we were due to fly out my mum passed away, it
wasn't unexpected, in fact the doctors had given her a week to live five
weeks previously. She had been in hospital for three months prior to
her death. My parents live a five-hundred-mile round trip from where
we live, we had been up a couple of weeks earlier with the family, but
I had felt prompted to go up again. We stayed with my dad on the
Friday and went to visit my mum on the Saturday, we drove home that
day and my mum passed away that night. Jean had spoken to my dad
about our up-and-coming trip knowing that in all probability something
would happen with my mum during that time. My dad encouraged us
to keep our plans no matter how things worked out. However, when
the time came my mum's funeral was going to be right in the middle of
our break, a trip that couldn't be changed or delayed, not because of
money but just through circumstances we would have to go on the
break or it wouldn't happen, after twenty years of waiting. The family
had the chance of two dates that would have accommodated me being
at the funeral but didn't take them because they couldn't get the hotel
they wanted for the funeral tea. Getting the right hotel was their
priority, more important to them than their son being there. I spoke to

my dad and as far as he was concerned the funeral plans couldn't be changed, we should just go and we would see him when we get back. I prayed about it and felt God give me a peace and release to go away.

Just six months later my dad passed away and on seeing his will I felt vindicated in not being at my mum's funeral. For whatever reason, one they never shared with me, I got the minimum they could legally give me, and my sister got the rest. The will was dated February 2011, long before my decision not to attend my mother's funeral. At my dad's funeral due to Covid-19 there were only four people at it, Jean and I being two of them, no cars and no hotel, only what was deemed necessary, family.

It would be too easy and perhaps a little trite to quote Jesus in Luke's Gospel as we were essentially going on holiday....

He said to another man, 'Follow me.' But he replied, 'Lord, first let me go and bury my father.' 60 Jesus said to him, 'Let the dead bury their own dead, but you go and proclaim the kingdom of God.'
Luke 9:59-60 (NIVUK)

But as we were to find out during the 'holiday' we were going to be there to 'proclaim the kingdom of God.'

The verse I did get was from Romans and it was one that gave me peace in what I was choosing to do. I felt I was being governed by the Spirit.

The mind governed by the flesh is death, but the mind governed by the Spirit is life and peace. Romans 8:6 (NIVUK)

Reactions to my decision were varied, mostly shock, some brave enough to tell me to my face, others I just have to take at face value that they meant what they said. The biggest shock was Jean's struggle with it, my parents and in particular my mum had never treated Jean well. She was really losing her peace over it. I eventually had to say to her the decision is mine to make and I have made it and I have peace from God about it. She submitted to my headship and was released into peace as well. So, on Monday 16th September we flew from Manchester to Toulouse.

On arrival at Toulouse airport (in 30degrees heat) we headed for Place du Capitole right in the city centre of Toulouse, I wanted to start from there with a meal at one of the street side restaurants. Driving on the wrong side of the road, in a busy city centre that I hadn't been in for nearly twenty years, in a car I had never driven before, (an Audi no less, the first time I had driven one) Jean said to me 'do you think this is a good idea?' I had hit the kerb a couple of times. But I pressed on, it made perfect sense to me. It was a main attraction, so it was well signposted, I knew it had a large underground car park, and I believed I was being guided by the Holy Spirit to start the journey well.

We got there in one piece and emerged from the car park into the sunshine and had a wonderful lunch French style (but without wine). It was amazing just sitting there in the sunshine with Jean, we were back where our journey with the Lord started and we were looking to reminisce, relax and recuperate for what God has got planned for the next season.

We left Toulouse and headed for Pibrac where we had stayed for four years, after heading off in the wrong direction we were soon back on track and arrived at Pibrac. We visited the church (which was open) and the basilica (which wasn't open). They now have a shop with items dedicated to St Germaine (see chapter 8) and we bought a few things before heading off to find our old house. Despite having lived there for four years we couldn't find it and eventually had to 'google' it. Having found it, it was a strange feeling, it was looking rather run down and sorry for itself. Neither of us felt any pangs to be back living there, that chapter was well and truly closed. We headed down to the Font de St Germaine where Jean received her healing back in 1999. At that time, it was very overgrown and almost unnoticeable but since 2012 they have restored it and it now overlooks a park. It is also still part of our walk 'Chemin des Anes' (see chapter 5). The visit here was more emotional, as the things of God now mean more to us than the material things.

We then headed towards Cornebarrieu past another old house which we rented for six months prior to buying our own. It had been looked after and looked nice sitting in the country with the sunshine on it, but it was just a house, somebody else's house. We headed to the village of Cornebarrieu where our old minister (Laurie, see chapter 6) lived, at least that's where he lived 19years ago when he dropped us of at the airport. We headed into the village not quite knowing where we were going, we hadn't been able to find our own house how would we find Laurie's?

As we drove in, there was a massive amount of new housing, a completely new estate and they were still adding to it. Just then Jean said to me 'I think we should be turning left about here' I took the next turning on the left and there right in front of us was the signpost for the street we were looking for. We dove on and found number 19, but would Laurie and Miriam still live here? I parked outside, and Jean said what are you going to do? I said I'm just going to have a look. Before I knew what was happening, I was knocking at the front door not sure who was going to answer. It was Laurie, Praise God! He was looking rather dishevelled and had aged, haven't we all? but there was more to his ageing it was unnatural. Jean heard me and as we went to the car to get her, she was coming out to meet us.

As we spoke to Laurie his story unfolded, he had burned out while in ministry and had come out a long time ago. He spent the first fifteen months labouring on a building site before doing some work for a year as a translator but more recently he hadn't worked for five years. In the in between years he had had two spells in a psychiatric ward where he had received electric shock treatment. (I was unaware they still used this but apparently it is used in cases of extreme depression). We spoke to him for a while in the presence of his wife Miriam and encouraged him by reminding them how much they had ministered to us over eighteen months while under their ministry and how it had given us a firm foundation. They were both due to go out, to separate places, had we been an hour later we would have missed them completely and not even knew they still lived in that house. We were leaving the area that night but had to come back this way to leave from Toulouse airport on the Friday. We swapped phone numbers and agreed to make arrangements to meet up on the Thursday.

We had booked hotel accommodation for the Tuesday, Wednesday and the Thursday but had nothing planned for the Monday night, we had previously cancelled our Monday night hotel as we felt it restricted us. After seeing Laurie, we felt our business in Toulouse was over and we headed down to the coast where we had booked a hotel for the Tuesday/Wednesday nights. Booking.com had no availability but we headed to the hotel in faith, we arrived about nine o'clock at night and, they had a room available for us, with a sea view, God is good. It was dark but the view was still amazing we could see the little light house at the end of the pier and the promenade in front of us was brightly lit and lined with palm trees. We went for a walk along the promenade and onto the pier it was just as we remembered it apart from one thing, us. The last time we were here we were a dead couple with a dead marriage heading for divorce. Jean was aware of it, I was just blindly stumbling along from one drink to the next. Jean had made tapes of some romantic songs and we had packed our best alcohol but there was nothing there. Jean felt empty I was empty. It was shortly after returning from this holiday that Jean found Jesus and became a Christian. I would follow later, helped and encouraged by Laurie's ministry. We were here now with Christ and with life, we looked forward to a different holiday and God was not about to let us down.

The blessing of the Lord makes one rich, And He adds no sorrow with it. Proverbs 10:22

The next morning, we were up and at the end of the pier to witness an amazing sunrise and the rest of the day was sunshine all the way. After a buffet breakfast we were on the beach all day, just soaking up the healing warmth of the sun's rays. We dressed for dinner and dined at the restaurant which overlooked the sea. The next day we had another super sunrise witnessed from our bedroom window. We spent the day relaxing and had a wonderful French lunch, yes you guessed it overlooking the beach. That afternoon we walked the beach, it went for miles and was a couple of hundred meters deep. We always walk along the sea having a paddle and we had done this yesterday and were doing it again today walking further than yesterday as we walked back, I said let's cut up here and we headed away from the beach. That was when we saw it, someone had made a homemade cross from some bleached driftwood. It was near a life guard station which was shut for the winter and as I poked my nosey way around it I came back to see Jean, she had found a crown of thorns lying on the sand next to the cross and had put it on it. It was so out of place and so out of our way it had to be the Spirit guiding us there.

The next morning Jean reflected on the cross with the crown of thorns, it was so unusual to see them like that, she felt God was asking her 'Where else have you seen this?' As she thought about it, it came to her, in St Gabriel's we have a large cross and someone has put a handmade crown of thorns around it. God is saying something to us in this, we believe He is saying that we are in the right place, he has taken us from Toulouse 20 years ago and has brought us to St Gabriel's for such a time as this. We are believing for God to do great things here and for His kingdom to advance.

The next morning, we again had a spectacular sunrise, just before the clouds rolled in and the rain started and it was time to go. We headed up the AutoRoute back to Toulouse and within a short while the sun was shining again. We made arrangements to meet Laurie at our hotel as we spelled out the address, he said 'Waw that's amazing'. We were at the Aerel Appart Hotel, 4 Rue Dieudonné Costes, Blagnac. Dieudonne translates in English to 'God given'; we were about to have a God given appointment with each other. The three of us (Jean, Laurie and me) sat in a lovely lounge in the hotel next door for hours, sharing, praying for and encouraging Laurie. He had been to hell and back and admitted that just a few days before meeting us he was wondering what was it all about and was his life worth anything. We saw the afternoon tea and coffee people come and go and the early evening drinkers arrive as we openly prayed and laid hands-on Laurie and encouraged him with everything the Holy Spirit was giving us, times when Laurie and Miriam had ministered to us in our despair and the foundations they helped to lay in our lives, when the Holy Spirit was moving mightily in his ministry. Five hours later when we parted, Laurie's countenance had changed. He thanked us for making Jesus real to him again. He had been asked to speak at the local American independent church the coming Sunday and had felt dry and as if he had nothing to offer and had been dreading it. We encouraged him that God was not finished with him and that God's anointing was still on him.

For the gifts and the calling of God are irrevocable. Romans 11:29

We flew back to England the next day and stopped off at a Steakhouse in Chester where I celebrated my 60th birthday with Jean, our daughter Kerry, son-in-law Andrew and two grandsons Rufus and Axel. It was a perfect way to end a perfect week.

We obviously had a heavy heart for Laurie but as I was writing this last chapter, he returned my call. I asked him how he got on with preaching he said it went well and people had come up to him and told him they had been touched, he even laughed. God is good.

As I finish this last chapter of this book, I look forward to the next book telling again of the goodness of God in the land of the living.

I thank God for the gift of my wife Jean who without her none of this would have been possible. Even to the point of her encouragement to write it.

JEAN, I LOVE YOU XXX.

May your fountain be blessed, and may you rejoice in the wife of your youth. Proverbs 5:18 (NIVUK)

I am indeed blessed, and only by the grace of God and the heart of a good wife, am I able to rejoice with the wife of my youth.

One couple's journey of faith and redemption told in 66 honest, real-life stories.

In 1998, whilst living in France, Alan and Jean McKinnell started on a journey that would change their lives forever. They were living in Toulouse, France which was a long way from Tarbolton, Scotland, the small village they were from. They had "made it" - Alan had a well-paid aerospace job, living in a lovely house with a swimming pool, and despite only being 38, retirement plans were already in place.

However, the masks they wore were cracking at an ever-increasing rate and they were about to face a reality check that would take them on a journey from near divorce to freedom in Christ. A journey that was only going to be completed because of God's unfailing grace.

This book is the story of that journey and what was waiting for them at the end of it. It contains the good, the bad and the ugliness of those years, told in a way that will help people struggling with life to know that no matter how dark life gets, there is a light at the end of the tunnel and his name is Jesus. The destination makes the pain of the journey so worthwhile.

Life is both good and challenging - enjoy the journey!